THE ART OF INTERROGATION

THE ART OF INTERROGATION

Mastering Techniques, Psychology, and Strategy in Modern Interrogation

K V THOMAS

JAICO PUBLISHING HOUSE

Ahmedabad Bangalore Chennai
Delhi Hyderabad Kolkata Mumbai

Published by Jaico Publishing House
A-2 Jash Chambers, 7-A Sir Phirozshah Mehta Road
Fort, Mumbai - 400 001
jaicopub@jaicobooks.com
www.jaicobooks.com

THE ART OF INTERROGATION
ISBN 978-93-48098-22-1

First Jaico Impression: 2025

Page design and layout by Inosoft Systems, Delhi

*Dedicated to all law enforcement and security personnel
who sacrificed their lives for the people and the nation.*

Contents

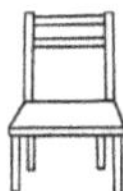

Abbreviations   ix

Preface   xi

1. History of Interrogation: From Ancient to Modern   1

2. Definition, Concept and Significance of Interrogation   10

3. Interview. Questioning. Interrogation   16

4. Interrogation: Signs from Body and Mind   26

5. Interrogation: Constitution and Laws   39

6. Planning, Preparation and Settings in Interrogation   50

7. Qualities and Skills of an Interrogator   56

8. Main Models of Interrogation   63

9. Types of Questions and the Art of Questioning   85

10. Actual Phase of Interrogation   97

11. Interrogation Techniques for Terrorists and Extremists 107

12. Interrogation Approaches and Techniques 117

13. Interrogation of Women and Juveniles 141

14. Science and Technology in Interrogation 147

15. Looking Ahead: How Can Interrogation Be Improved? 163

Notes 174

Bibliography 186

About the Author 189

Abbreviations

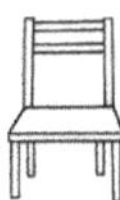

AI	Artificial Intelligence
BAI	Behavioural Analysis Interview
CIA	Central Intelligence Agency
CVSA	Computer Voice Stress Analysis
CRC	Convention on the Rights of Children
CQT	Controlled Question Test
DM	Defence Mechanisms
EEG	Electroencephalography
EGG	Electrogastrogram
EIT	Enhanced Interrogation Techniques
ECHR	European Convention on Human Rights
FBI	Federal Bureau of Investigations
fMRI	Functional Magnetic Resonance Imaging
GKT	Guilty Knowledge Test
IBC	Interpersonal Behaviour Cycle

ICCPR	International Convention on Civil and Political Rights
ISIS	Islamic State of Iraq and Syria
LET	Lashkar-e-Taiba
LTM	Long-Term Memory
MEG	Magnetic Encephalography
MERMER	Memory and Encoding Related Multifaceted Encephalographic Response
MI	Motivational Interviewing
NHRC	National Human Rights Commission
NPA	National Police Academy (of Japan)
NGO	Non-governmental Organization
OODA(Loop)	Observe, Orient, Decide and Act
PEI	Position Emission Tomography
POW	Prisoners of War
PKAP	Practical Kinesic Analysis Phase
PEACE	Preparation and Planning, Engage and Explain, Account, Closure and Evaluate
RPM	Rationalization, Projection and Minimization
SM	Sensory Memory
STM	Short-Term Memory
SERE	Survival, Evasion, Resistance, Escape (Training)
SVA	Statement Validity Analysis
SHRC	State Human Rights Commission
UNDHR	United Nations Declaration Human Rights

Preface

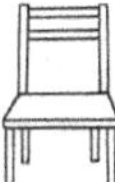

IN THE AFTERMATH OF 9/11, when Guantanamo Bay, Abu Ghraib, Bagram and other black sites of the Central Intelligence Agency (CIA) of the US have created waves in an international polity with divergent views and arguments, the theme of interrogation has taken centre stage in the fight against global terrorism. Interrogation, which was previously identified as a potential tool in criminal investigations, has now been accepted as one of the most effective mechanisms to generate actionable intelligence pertaining to terrorists, extremists and other groups endangering peace and order in society. The bourgeoning role of interrogation—both in law enforcement and national security architecture—has prompted me to delve deeper into how interrogation can be effectively used in the field of criminal investigations and to generate tactical and strategic intelligence. While my conceptual foundation builds upon authentic works by eminent scholars and criminologists, and peer-reviewed researches, many of the techniques and approaches to interrogation incorporated in the book are based on my own experience in the field and on inputs by police interrogators and prominent criminologists. I have also included a number of case studies to help readers of this book better understand and appreciate the art of interrogation.

Chapter 1 traces the history of interrogation from the pharaohs of Egypt to the twenty-first century when Enhanced Interrogation Techniques (EIT) have been used by the US in their fight against al-Qaeda. Though the methods and techniques of interrogation have varied across, torture, in one form or another, has always existed to extract confessions or elicit the truth from the suspects or accused. The concept, definitions and significance of interrogation are discussed in Chapter 2. While the main emphasis of law enforcement-related interrogation is on finding answers in relation to a crime, strategic or intelligence interrogation is meant to secure actionable intelligence from suspects or persons in custody. In both cases, false confessions have become an international problem, with wide ramifications in the criminal justice process.

Research indicates that accusatorial methods increase the likelihood of false confessions as compared with information gathering methods.

Chapter 3 discusses the significance of the pre-interrogation interview and questioning in any criminal investigation. Non-accusatory interviewing of the suspects is crucial to collect important leads connected with the crime, eliminate improbable suspects and identify potential witnesses who are of immense help in strengthening prosecution evidence. Case references further discuss the recording of witness statements—a crucial aspect of criminal investigations. The interrelationships between the human mind and body, as established by the Oriental school of thought and the Western philosophers and modern psychoanalysts, can be found in Chapter 4, especially as they relate to interrogation. Proper identification of verbal and non-verbal responses, including the suspect's facial expressions, is vital in deciphering deceit and lies. In this chapter, I catalogue such major responses and corresponding inferences for the ready reference of interrogators and investigators.

In Chapter 5, case studies demonstrate the constitutional and legal safeguards for the accused such as the right against self-incrimination or the right to silence or the Miranda clause as enshrined in the constitution and legal system of various countries such as the US, UK, Australia, Canada, and India. Inevitably, while adhering to such constitutional and legal parameters, the success of any interrogation depends on preparation, planning and settings—which are discussed in Chapter 6. Interrogators or investigators need to collect as much detail as possible about the crime and the suspect so as to enable them to work out proper strategy and techniques during the actual interrogation.

The qualities and skills of interrogators play a crucial role in the success of an interrogation. These qualities are analyzed in detail in Chapter 7, which focuses on the findings of eminent criminologists like Hans Gross and Hans Scharff. Working with experts helps to develop many of these skills and qualities. In this regard, a better understanding of the different models of interrogation, and participation in such interrogation processes, would enrich one's experience. In Chapter 8, the main models like Reid, Kinesic and PEACE are discussed in detail, along with certain loopholes and drawbacks such as the misclassification error leading to false confessions, as happened in sensational cases such as the Stephanie Crowe murder.

Chapter 10 describes the actual phase of interrogation and how interrogators build up a rapport with the suspect or accused and use different techniques to elicit the truth. The type of questions and the art of questioning, as outlined in Chapter 9, are of considerable importance in maintaining a proper ambience during the interrogation. Different approaches and techniques adopted by interrogators during interrogations, including those of terrorists and extremists, are discussed in great detail in Chapters 11 and 12, with case studies and examples. Techniques such as Rationalization, Projection and Minimization, commonly known as RPM, are meant to inactivate or neutralize defence mechanisms (DMs) used by the accused to conceal their crime. The basic principle is that an interrogation would not be successful so long as these DMs remain active in the mind of the accused.

As in any other sphere, science and technology play a leading role in the field of interrogation. Chapter 14 discusses scientific aids to interrogation such as the Polygraph, P-300 Brain Mapping test, narcoanalysis, Computer Voice Stress Analysis (CVSA) and other innovative technologies along with their legal status and implications. The concluding chapter highlights a number of insights and suggestions—organizational, personal, legislative and logistical—to revamp and reform the tool of interrogation so as to use it more effectively to meet the new challenges in the fields of criminal investigation and national security.

K V Thomas

1

History of Interrogation

From Ancient to Modern

THE HISTORY OF INTERROGATION, just like the history of crime, goes back to the genesis of the human race. The story of Abel and Cain, as narrated in the Bible's Book of Genesis 4: 8-11[1] relates the offence of murder. Enraged by jealousy and hatred of God's blessings to his younger brother Abel, Cain, the son of Adam and Eve, kills Abel and conceals his body in a field. God asks Cain, "Where is Abel your brother?" and Cain's defiant response, "I do not know; am I my brother's keeper?" reflects a suspect's approach to try to conceal his guilt. His arrogant words, "am I my brother's keeper?" can be interpreted as a clear verbal signal, reflecting Cain's guilty feelings. The Lord corners Cain with the next question, "What have you done? The voice of your brother's blood is crying to me from the ground." The Lord, here, behaves like a professional interrogator and shares a piece of evidence in order to expedite the process of Cain's admission of crime.

The Book of Kings I[2] (3:16-28) recounts the story of two mothers living in the same house, both with an infant son. When one of the babies died in his sleep, they came to King Solomon, each claiming the other boy as her own. The second mother said, "My son is alive and your son is dead." The first mother responded, "It is not so! Your son is the dead one and my son is the living one." Solomon announced his judgment: the baby would be cut in two, each woman to receive half. One mother did not contest the ruling, declaring that if she could not have the baby then neither of them could, but the other begged Solomon, "Give the baby to her, just don't kill him!" The king declared the second woman the true mother, as a mother would even give up her baby if that was necessary to save its life. This famous story of King Soloman highlights many common techniques used in an interrogation such as bluffing (cutting the baby into two) and picking up on verbal and non-verbal clues, such as the compassion and the cruelty reflected in the words of the deceitful and the innocent woman.

In ancient times, many ingenious methods were used to elicit the truth during interrogations. According to *Pyramid Texts*, pharoahs in Egypt, who were described as God's representatives on earth, employed inhuman methods while dealing with law violators. During the trial of the infamous Ramesside tomb robberies,[3] the accused were beaten with rods in the presence of Nesuaman, the police chief, to identify the real culprits. In ancient China, suspects were asked to hold uncooked rice in their mouths while they were interrogated. Then, they were directed to spit out the rice. The innocent, whose mouth contained saliva, spit out wet globular pieces of rice. But the deceptive individuals, whose mouth had become dry due to physiological responses to suppress the fear of detection, spit out dry rice kernels. Similarly, in many parts of Africa, ostrich eggs were used to detect the innocent and the guilty. Those who were suspected of crime were asked to pass an ostrich egg to one another while being interrogated, and if one dropped it during the process, he or she would be identified as guilty. This was based on the assumption that the guilty person would be susceptible to nervousness and fear of detection and would be more likely to drop the egg.

Ancient India has a rich history of such ingenious practices. Around 500 BC, the sacred donkey was used as a means of detecting deception. A donkey was kept in a tent and each suspect was asked to enter the tent and pull the donkey's tail. The accused were informed that the donkey had a direct link to the Divine and would bray when its tail was pulled by the guilty. While the innocent cooly entered the tent and pulled the donkey's tail, the guilty person feared detection and didn't pull the tail. The donkey had no divine powers but its tail was secretly smeared with lampblack, the mark of which was clear on the hands of all innocent persons who pulled the tail. Obviously, the guilty had no such marks as they feared to pull the tail. In *Chanakya Niti*,[4] the concepts of saam (advise and ask), daam (to offer and buy), dand (to punish) and bhed (exploiting the differences) were described by Acharya Chanakya during the fourth to third century BC and they have been widely used during interrogations. The whole concept revolves around the exploitation of the suspect's secrets after ascertaining his or her personality, weakness, priorities, expectations and intentions through critical analysis of the answers given during the interrogation. Just like Chanakya, Birbal, the advisor and chief commander of the Mughal emperor Akbar, excelled in the art of identifying the accused from the innocent by using his wit and gift of gab.

During the middle ages, interrogators adopted torture and humiliation to extract confessions or to punish the guilty. With no legal regulations, medieval Europe witnessed the most horrific and inhumane methods of torture, which included: rat torture, iron chair, the Judas cradle, thumbscrew, flogging, the cage and the iron maiden. Many of these methods were extensively used during the Spanish and Medieval Inquisitions[5] carried out by the Church to identify and punish heretics. Around one lakh people were the victims of such torture and killing. The Salem witch trials[6] (1692-93)—a series of hearings and prosecution of people accused of witchcraft in colonial Massachusetts in the US—were one of the most notorious examples of the lapses in due process in areas of law enforcement. Of the 200 odd accused, 30 were found guilty and 19 of them executed. It was perhaps the first time that defendants and witness testimony had a permanent record of interrogation.

The sixteenth and seventeenth centuries continued to witness torture and an inhuman treatment of prisoners during interrogation. Under the reign of Louis XIV of France, torture was allowed as a form of interrogation mainly to extract confessions from the accused (Question Préparatoire) and to obtain the names and details about accomplices (Question Préalable)[7]. Two common forms of judicial torture were strappado and the brodequins.[8] In strappado, the accused's hands were bound and then the accused was lifted into the air by a pulley system. During the interrogation, the accused would be dropped from where they were previously suspended, only to then be caught by the pulley system just prior to hitting the ground. In the brodequins, boot-like restraints were placed on the calves of the accused and pressed tighter and tighter together during interrogation. Other common forms of torture were water torture, where individuals were forced to consume large quantities of water during interrogation, as well as sleep deprivation, where the accused were forced to stay awake for around 40 hours. Such methods were used extensively not only in France but also in many European and other countries where dictators were in power.

The rise of dictators like Adolf Hitler (Germany), Benito Mussolini (Italy), Joseph Stalin (Soviet Union), Mao Zedong (China) and similar rulers in East Europe, Latin America, Africa and Asia during the nineteenth and twentieth centuries led to the extensive use of new techniques of interrogation that mainly targeted dissidents and adversaries. Their police and secret services were given a free hand to deal with such elements using extreme methods during detention in concentration camps and jail. The dissidents and progressive intellectuals like Aleksandr Solzhenitsyn of erstwhile Soviet Union have given vivid accounts of such methods and practices in their memoirs and literary works. Perhaps the best example is an extract from Solzhenitsyn's famous work, *The Gulag Archipelago*. He wrote that, "prisoners would have their skulls squeezed within iron rings; that human beings would be lowered into acid baths; that they would be trussed up naked to be bitten by ants and bedbugs; that ramrods heated over primus stoves would be thrust up their anal canals (the "secret brand"); that a man's genitals would be slowly crushed beneath the toe of a jackboot; and that in the luckiest possible circumstances, prisoners would be tortured by being kept from sleeping for a week, by thirst, and by being beaten to a bloody pulp."[9]

Even the countries strongly committed to democracy and rule of law adopted different shades of torture, deceit and trickery during interrogation. The New York City Detective Bureau headed by Inspector Thomas Brynes from 1880-1895 extensively used such practices leading to considerable public criticism. The Wickersham Commission of 1931,[10] which examined law enforcement practices in the US, confirmed the widespread use of third-degree methods during interrogation and recommended modern methods and practices in the field of interrogation. In Brown v. Mississippi,[11] the US Supreme Court denounced third-degree deceit and trickery during interrogation.

Two major developments that influenced interrogation methods and techniques in the twentieth century were the Second World War and the USA's protracted war in Vietnam, Latin America, Afghanistan and Iraq. In the Phoenix Project,[12] which was launched in Vietnam during the 1960s, a number of methods such as electric shock, water torture, hanging from ceilings were used during the interrogation of Vietnamese soldiers and rebels. In many places, specially designed interrogation chambers were constructed where such methods, including the rape of suspected women, were used to break the suspects. A similar clandestine project named Plan Condor[13] was launched in Latin America in 1975. Under this project, Latin American military leaders used extreme methods during the interrogation of their opponents and dissidents.

During World War II, there was widespread use of third-degree interrogation. The major powers like the US, Germany and Japan developed different interrogation strategies for various types of prisoners and civilians in occupied territories, violating the provisions of the Geneva Convention. For example, the Germans regarded Bolsheviks or Communists undeserving of Prisoners of War (POW) status under the Geneva Convention[14] and treated them inhumanely in their methods of interrogation under the supervision of their security police and Gestapo. Their third-degree methods included a simple diet (bread and water), hard bunk, dark cell, deprivation of sleep, exhaustive drilling and flogging. However, influenced by the lobbying of civil liberties organizations and voluntary outfits like the International Red Cross that focus on the covenants of the Geneva Convention, countries like the US and Germany have explored new strategies for the interrogation of POWs.

Hanns Scharff,[15] master interrogator of Nazi Germany, was the innovator in such endeavors. Scharff was responsible for interrogating the airmen of Allied forces captured during bombing raids over Europe. Instead of adopting third-degree methods, he employed a different interrogation strategy based on a sophisticated intelligence-gathering system cataloguing the minutiae of everyday life on the Allied bomber bases. In most cases, the POWs being interrogated never realized that their words, small talk or otherwise, were important pieces of the mosaic that Scharff was constructing for the benefit of Germany's war efforts. He was also the architect of the new interrogation model introduced by the US Army and allied establishments. Just like Scharff, Major Sherwood F Moran,[16] who was assigned to interrogate the captured Japanese in the Pacific theatre of World War II, adopted soft-cold methods to establish rapport with the prisoners during interrogation. His rich experience and understanding of Japanese culture, customs and language, by virtue of his long stay in the country as a missionary enabled him to successfully undertake these assignments. Moran's message to modern-day interrogators was, "Know their (the prisoners') language, know their culture and treat the captured enemy as a human being."

Such new interrogation strategies gained further momentum

during the post-World War II period. The adoption of the United Nations Declaration of Human Rights (UNDHR) in 1948 was a landmark development in this arena, as it underlined certain crucial factors closely intertwined with interrogation. For example, the declaration held that no one shall be subjected to torture, cruel, inhumane or degrading treatment or punishment (Article 5) or arbitrary arrest, detention or exile (Article 9). The equality for law and the equal protection of law, as enshrined in Article 7 of the declaration essentially constituted a crucial element of interrogation in stating that the rights and safeguards of the accused or suspect should be protected while eliciting the truth. The enactment of a number of Conventions such as the Geneva Convention on the rights of Prisoners of War (1949), the International Covenant on Civil and Political Rights (1966), the Convention against Torture and Other Cruel Treatment and Punishment (1987) by the UN, and their ratification by the comity of nations has substantially influenced the functioning of police and other law enforcement establishments across the world. Added to this was the organized campaign and propaganda by leading non-governmental organizations (NGOs) and civil liberties organizations such as Amnesty International and Human Rights Watch against torture, custodial violence, third-degree and excesses and misuse of power by state super-structures, especially law enforcement agencies. The dissemination of such ideals gained further momentum with the Vienna Declaration of Human Rights (1993)[17]. A related development was the increased application of science and technology in the field of interrogation.

But everything changed drastically in the aftermath of the September 11, 2001 attacks on the US. The global war against terrorism became the main task of many nations that gave unchecked power to their security and investigation agencies to eliminate menace, even if they had to resort to extreme measures. The US interrogation camps at Guantanamo Bay (Cuba), Abu Ghraib (Iraq) and Bagram (Afghanistan) liberally used such measures, nicknamed Enhanced Interrogation Techniques, reminiscent of extreme interrogation methods practiced by the US forces in Vietnam and other places in the twentieth century. The US military training program Survival, Evasion, Resistance, Escape Training (SERE) that taught survival skills, how to evade capture, recovery and surviving captivity was reverse engineered into harsh interrogation techniques against suspected terror-detenus. Some of these methods included stress positions, beating, temperature manipulation, waterboarding (mock drowning), threats of harm to person or family or friends, sleep deprivation, sensory bombardment using light and sound, violent shaking, sexual humiliation and prolonged isolation and sensory deprivation. When the US administration legally sanctified those methods in the laudable task of fighting global terrorism, more and more countries followed suit and shifted the balance of law and administrative practices towards the sole theme of national security. As terrorism and extremism continue as major challenges to global peace and security in the twenty-first century, security and law enforcement agencies continue to resort to such interrogation techniques in the fight against terrorism and organized crime.

2

Definition, Concept and Significance of Interrogation

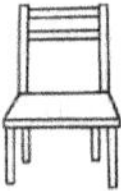

INTERROGATION IS THE PROCESS OF SYSTEMATIC QUESTIONING OF A suspect or person in order to elicit truth about his or her offense or other illegal activities. In the other words, it is the process of obtaining information that an individual does not or may not want to provide to others, especially investigators. Thus, from the criminal justice angle, interrogation is defined as "systematic efforts by Law enforcement investigators to prove, disprove or corroborate information relevant to criminal investigation using direct questioning under controlled environment."[18] As the definition indicates, the purpose of law enforcement related interrogation is to search for answers in relation to a crime; to fill in the blanks or find the missing links in a case as well as to exonerate those wrongly or falsely implicated in a case. "Not only Law enforcement agencies, but a myriad of organizations entrusted with National security or strategic matters use interrogation to secure actionable intelligence from person(s) or suspects in their custody."[19]

In the case of conflicts or battles, tactical interrogation—real-time interrogation to collect on-the-ground actionable intelligence—is helpful for the combatants to make decisive successful moves against adversaries. US forces that have fought influential wars across the globe excel in the art of tactical interrogation using coercive and non-coercive methods. On the other hand, strategic interrogation focuses on broader knowledge about enemy forces—their strength, deployment, logistics, modern weaponry, sensitive infrastructure and morale. POWs are the best sources of the most useful tactical and strategic intelligence. Steven Kleinman[20] has written a brilliant study of various strategic interrogation methods adopted by the US in World War II. Similarly, in the ongoing global war on terror, tactical and strategic interrogations are primarily meant to generate operational and strategic intelligence on terrorism's critical centres of gravity such as financing, transportation, logistics, communications and safe havens. The best example is the interrogation of David Coleman Headley, a US citizen partly of Pakistani descent, who was involved in the November 2008 Mumbai terrorist attacks and a subsequent proposed attack on a Denmark newspaper. A joint interrogation of Headley could unravel vital intelligence on al-Qaeda, Lashkar-e-Toiba (LET) and their affiliates across different continents, their clandestine operations, conduits, financial sources, interlinkages and communication channels. On many instances, harsh interrogation methods have been used to elicit actionable intelligence from detained terror elements, as in the case of the interrogation of al-Qaeda suspects in various

US interrogation centres at Guantanamo Bay or Bagram. Such interrogation techniques stand in contrast to the different facets of interrogation of suspects involved in criminal or similar offenses.

The nature and objectives of law enforcement interrogations differ significantly from those in tactical or strategic interrogations. Unlike a police interrogation, strategic or intelligence interrogation does not aim to make the suspect incriminate himself as a means of bringing him to trial. Confessions or admissions of complicity are not ends in themselves but means for the acquisition or elicitation of more information or intelligence. In a nut shell, while law enforcement attempts to understand the past, strategic or tactical interrogation attempts to probe the future. The table below summarizes the major differences between these areas of interrogation with particular reference to their objectives and priorities.

Table I: Law Enforcement vs Strategic or Intelligence Interrogation

Factors	Law Enforcement	Strategic/Intelligence
Objective	Conviction	Understanding
Standard	Legal method	Analytical methods
Limits	Evidence-based	None
Protection	Fifth Amendment/Miranda	None
Confession	Considerable value	Relative value

An analysis of the critical factors of law enforcement and strategic interrogations reveals that they have numerous areas of commonality but are critically different in the areas of strategy, timing and focus. Law enforcement interrogators seek to obtain a confession from the suspect so as to ensure conviction of the accused. For them, collection of further accurate or useful information or intelligence from a possibly cognizant suspect is secondary. Thus, these interrogators are required to fulfil legal parameters and due process, whereas those engaged in strategic interrogation enjoy a greater degree of flexibility—both in application and practice of interrogation.

As interrogation is an essential component of investigation, investigators or agencies should adhere to certain procedural standards and rules pertaining to due process. If agencies do not comply with due process or violate any procedural rules, the results of the interrogation, such as the questions and the responses, will not be admissible in court as evidence. Thus, proper interrogation of suspects is particularly important in ensuring convictions against the guilty and exonerating those wrongly implicated. In criminal interrogations, there are two general approaches—information gathering and accusatorial. The information gathering approach, more prevalent in the United Kingdom, New Zealand, Australia and elsewhere, is characterized by rapport building, truth seeking and active listening. On the other hand, in the accusatorial approach, which is more common in the United States and Canada, the main focus is on accusation, confrontation, psychological manipulation and the disallowing of denials. Both these methods are practiced in India depending upon the nature of suspects and detainees and the nature of offenses. These interrogation methods had been subjected to serious debates and criticisms in the wake of false confessions or admissions leading to convictions.

As the elicitation of false confessions has become an international problem with wider ramifications in the criminal justice process, a number of empirical studies have been conducted in different countries to better understand the issue. Certain studies, such as

Meissner and Russano[21] demonstrated that accusatorial methods increase the likelihood of a false confession, while information gathering methods protect the innocent yet preserve interrogators' ability to elicit confessions from guilty persons. Despite the wide application of accusatorial methods, their confession rate is substantially lower (around 15%) in the US than in the UK. However, Richard Leo found that "in the US almost two-thirds (64.29%) of the interrogations produced a successful result."[22] Leo also established that the frequency of full confessions during interrogations was around 24%; partial admission accounted for 18% and elicitation of incriminating inputs was at 23%. In around 36% of cases, no incriminating inputs could be gathered during interrogation. According to Leo, an interrogation is rated as successful if the suspect or accused provided at least some incriminating inputs to the interrogators.

A number of factors influence the nature of the confession. A suspect's background, particularly his or her psychological vulnerabilities, and the physiological accusatorial methods are the two major factors. It has been generally established that juveniles or minors are more susceptible to admissions. A 1970 US study[23] found that 42.9% of suspects under the age of 25 in Colorado made confessions under police interrogation compared to 18.2% of older suspects. However, researchers are divided on the issue of gender. Several British and US researchers[24] have found no gender differences with regard to the rate of admissions and denials. On the other hand, other researchers[25] found a significant gender difference, with females confessing more commonly than males (73% admission rate of females versus 52% of males). Other factors such as ethnic differences or previous conviction also influence confessions.

Just like other spheres of the criminal justice process, the art of interrogation has been undergoing innovation with creative ideas and practices. The effectiveness of strategic interrogations has come under intense criticism when the stories of Enhanced Interrogation Techniques in Vietnam, Iraq and Afghanistan had highlighted bitter episodes of the use of torture and other inhumane methods during interrogation. Serious questions have been raised on the use and efficacy of such techniques for collecting intelligence or information. In many countries like Canada and the US, criminologists and psychoanalysts had developed special techniques of interrogation. For example, the Reid technique of interrogation is a fairly well-known method that is widely followed in the US. The highest courts of law in the US and other developed nations have endorsed the validity of Reid as a legal measure for action. Influenced by Article 6 of the European Convention on Human Rights (ECHR), many Western countries have banned close-ended or confirmatory questions and deception during interrogation. Other countries, such as the United Kingdom, Norway, New Zealand and Australia, have amended their interrogation practices to employ information gathering methods of interrogation. Japan has continuously engaged in developing more and more creative ways of interrogation. The National Police Academy of Japan effectively disseminate such techniques to the investigators across the country. In many advanced countries like the US, UK and Israel, Artificial intelligence (AI) and robotics have stepped into the arena of interrogation for better interpretation and analysis of verbal and non-verbal responses from the suspects in order to arrive at the right conclusions. Perhaps, slowly and steadily, such modern technologies and devices may replace human interrogators who are definitely limited as successful lie detectors.

3

Interview. Questioning. Interrogation

CRIMINAL INVESTIGATION ESSENTIALLY CONSTITUTES the collection, collation, analysis and validation of data or evidence connected with an offense or crime. An investigator's tasks include identification of physical evidence, gathering information, collection and protection of evidence, interviewing of suspects and witnesses, identification of suspects, search, arrest, interrogation of the accused and laying charges. A deep understanding of these steps, and a professional approach are key for a good investigator and essential for the success of the investigation.

Any investigation commences with the process of enquiry, which may be open or secret. While the investigators undertake open enquiry connected with the crime by visiting the place of occurrence or crime scene, the detectives or those belonging to specialized wings such as Crime or Vigilance conduct secret enquiries to collect leading clues or evidence helpful for the investigation. After the initial enquiry, they start the process of gathering verbal responses from a suspect or possible suspects or persons who can throw more light on the offense.

The interview, questioning and interrogation are the three distinct phases of such a verbal interaction by the investigators. When and how each process should be undertaken during the information or evidence gathering process differs across cases. Understanding the correct procedures and the legal parameters of these processes is vital in criminal investigations.

Interviewing is the first and lowest level of interaction with a possible suspect. This process is basically meant to ascertain the involvement of a person in a particular crime. Simply by obtaining statements from such a person, the investigator may arrive at a conclusion. If any piece of evidence—direct or circumstantial—is unearthed during this process, the investigator has reasonable grounds to suspect a person's involvement and the suspect can be detained for specific questioning.

Questioning is the next level of interaction. The investigator should continue to offer the suspect an opportunity to disclose more information that may be exculpatory, enabling him or her to establish their innocence. On the other hand, if further disclosures are full of contradictions and go against already established evidence in relation to the offense under investigation, the person is arrested after ensuring the due process of law.

Interrogation is the next stage of the investigation, in which the accused is subjected to systematic and detailed questioning to elicit truth or concrete evidence. An example can help us better understand these processes.

Let us imagine a shabbily dressed youth standing by himself near a city bus shelter during the wee hours, around 300-400 meters away from a bank ATM that was broken and looted. Following a crime alert, a police patrol comes across the youth on their way to the scene of crime. They can naturally suspect him because of his presence at odd hours near the crime scene. The process of interview commences and the patrol quizzes him about his identity and other details and the reason for his presence at the spot. He is obligated to furnish these details to the patrol chief.

If his explanations are not convincing, the patrol chief can detain and question the young man in connection with the crime. He should continue to offer the youth an opportunity to disclose information that would prove his innocence. Had the youth answered the questions about his presence there convincingly, it would have greatly reduced the suspicion against him. The confirmation of his claims would eliminate him as a suspect and result in his release. On the other hand, when the patrol finds contradictions within his disclosures and there is additional physical evidence implicating his involvement in the crime, the youth needs to be arrested and subjected to thorough interrogation to bring out the whole truth, including his accomplices and modus operandi of the crime. Even if they ultimately find that the youth is innocent, they can use the interviewing process to elicit clues or leads that would help the investigation. The major differences between interview, questioning and interrogation are tabulated below.

In criminal investigations, a non-accusatory pre-interrogation interview is important for a number of reasons. First, as innocent suspects are the best sources for investigative clues, a proper interview can gather a lot of useful information about other suspects, modus operandi, the crime scene, motives and associates. Similarly, the factual narration of events from victims of offenses

Table II: Interview, Questioning and Interrogation: Differences at a Glance

Interview	Questioning	Interrogation
First phase of investigation	Second stage of investigation	Final and serious stage
Suspect or witness	Suspect or possible suspect	Confirmed suspect
No arrest or detention	Detained for questioning	Arrested
No links established	Reasonable grounds for doubt	Elicit more evidence
Non-accusatory	Semi-accusatory with caution	Accusatory
Dialogue—question and answer	Modified dialogue with an aim	More of a monologue
Investigative/behavioral leads	Investigative/behavioral leads	Elicit the truth
Assess truthfulness	Assess truthfulness	Obtain confession
Conversation with a purpose	Prove innocence or involvement	Incriminating inputs
Would not withhold information	Would try to withhold information	Reluctant/non-cooperative
More talk by interviewee	Motivate interviewee to talk	More talk by interviewer
Ascertain role	Release or detention	Confession/admission

such as simple or grievous hurt, attempt to murder or molestation would allow the investigators to narrow down the number of suspects for interview and help to identify the actual culprits.

The interview of multiple suspects in sensational cases and the proper recording of their statements will enhance the reliability of the prosecution's evidence during trial. Such measures, to a great extent, would blunt the weapon of the defense when they attack the prosecution's evidence.

More important are the advantages of the pre-interrogation interview during custodial interrogation of the suspect. It would provide the interrogators, in advance, some vital clues on the type and characteristics of the suspect, based on which they can make reasonable guesses about the suspect's probable attitude towards the interrogation. A preliminary estimate of whether the suspect will be cooperative or recalcitrant is of great help in planning sound strategy in dealing with him or her during the interrogation. Accordingly, available assets such as the number of interrogators, linguistic experts or interpreters and analysts can be efficiently and judiciously deployed to ensure the success of the interrogation. The interview also enables the interrogators to determine the behavioural baseline of the suspect against which they can assess the suspect's subsequent change of behaviour and responses (both verbal and non-verbal). This is particularly useful to the interrogators to arrive at crucial conclusions on the veracity of the suspect's statements. Next, by identifying contradictions and lies from the suspect's initial narration of events during the interview, the investigators can corner the person with the right techniques. Finally, the pre-interrogation interview functions as the first contact between interrogator and suspect and, given its non-accusatory nature, offers a fertile opportunity to establish rapport with the suspect. Empirical studies on rapport-building during investigative interviews found that in almost half of the interviews with suspects, such rapport was lacking and in those that did, the skills left much to be desired. In a unique study of 142 real police interviews with individuals suspected of benefit fraud, Walsh and Bull (2012) found that interviewers who were able to establish and maintain a rapport throughout the interview could obtain five times more than the outcome achieved by their counterparts bereft of such skills (42% vs 8%). The study also revealed that opportunities to build rapport with suspects through strategies such as patient listening or empathy in the initial stages of the interview were often not taken and that where it had been established, the same could not be maintained throughout the interview.

Proper interviewing of probable suspects enables investigators to identify witnesses who are vital to the successful investigation of the case and conviction of the accused. *Black's Law Dictionary* defines a witness as "one who sees, knows or vouches for something or one who gives testimony, under oath or affirmation." A witness in a criminal case involves one who tells what he or she saw, experienced or heard about a crime. As a witness, they are only allowed to talk about events that they know about personally.

Experienced investigators, very often, can spot ideal witnesses from among the probable suspects who are subjected to interview and subsequently turn out to be innocent. Behavioural information is the main parameter for identifying them as potential witnesses. Based on behaviour patterns and their overall personality, witnesses are broadly classified as: a) honest and co-operative b) silent c) reluctant or suspicious d) bashful or timid e) hostile and deceitful f) talkative or boastful and g) those influenced by extraneous forces or incentives. The investigation officer adopts different approaches or strategies to establish rapport with possible witnesses depending upon their unique qualities or personality. Persons who appear to be hostile or deceitful by nature should not be listed as witnesses, nor their statements taken as evidence.

Investigation officers need to adhere to some basic principles or guidelines while interviewing witnesses. Before the interview commences, they should be thoroughly acquainted with the case and the background or biosocial status of the interviewee. For that purpose, the crime scene visit or preliminary enquiry is vital. When the investigator commences the interview, he should reveal his identity and the nature of the interview. He should explain to the witness why he or she is being interviewed and that the statement is being recorded in connection with the investigation of that particular case. The investigator should also apprise the witness of his or her duty to provide accurate facts.

Building a rapport is the cornerstone of the entire interview process. By using the right tactics, investigators can build a good relationship with the witnesses. For that purpose, they should be treated with dignity and courtesy. Investigators should not use intimidation or coercion to influence the witnesses in line with the investigator's story. At the outset, they should be relieved of stress and strain with an assurance that the interview is voluntary and they can end it at any time. In the case of timid witnesses, they should be assured of due protection against retaliation from any side. To buttress their confidence, the investigator can assure them that their statements will be kept confidential, with a suggestion that they too keep the interview confidential. Moreover, for proper investigation and adducing of evidence and a successful prosecution, witness protection and ensuring the confidentiality of statements have become crucial, especially when there are organized moves from various corners to influence prosecution witnesses in sensational cases. Once important prosecution witnesses are won over or made hostile, the case is weakened and the culprits would go scot-free.

In order to get the true version of the committed crime and to augment prosecution evidence, investigators have to adopt a natural style of interview. Deductive funnel questions are the most suitable to elicit maximum evidence. Usually, this method of questioning commences with open-ended questions meant to foster narration on the part of the witness, followed by more closed questions such as indicator questions, identification questions, multiple choice questions and leading (yes or no) questions to get specific details. Investigators should consciously avoid legal or investigative jargon, which very often confuses illiterate or semi-literate witnesses. They should not give any indication to the witness about their findings or their impressions related to the case, nor divulge their future course of action. It is better to take written note of the witness statements throughout the interview so that investigators do not miss any crucial revelations.

Once the questioning is complete, the investigator can read out the witness statement to ensure its accuracy. During this stage, the witness can add or delete anything that he or she finds relevant or absent. The investigator needs to assess the statement in order to ascertain its evidentiary value for the prosecution. In case there are half-baked or incomplete statements from reluctant or timid witnesses, the investigator should try to get useful tips or details about other possible witnesses who can provide direct evidence or connect the missing links of evidence in the case. Experienced interrogators continue to maintain rapport with potential witnesses by making arrangements for future contact. On many occasions, they are briefed so that they know they can cater any information at a later stage that they deem fit to strengthen the prosecution's case.

At the same time, merely enlisting a large number of witnesses to augment the prosecution evidence does not serve the investigation unless the evidence so collected is incorporated with meticulous precision, plugging the likely legal or procedural loopholes that may come up during the trial of the sensational cases. On many occasions, failure to do so has ultimately derailed the entire prosecution, leading to the acquittal of the accused or commutation of their punishment by upper courts.

Perhaps the best example for this is the rape and murder case of a 23-year-old girl travelling in a ladies' compartment of a passenger train, in Kerala, in February 2011. A team of competent investigators completed the investigation in record time. The prosecution accused a single person in the crime—a beggar-like vagabond who, on seeing the girl alone in the compartment, trespassed into it, attacked her by brutally hitting her head many times against the walls of the coach, caused grievous injuries and threw her from the train on the railway tracks and raped her. She succumbed to her serious injuries after struggling for five days in the hospital. Backed by physical witnesses and corroborated by post-mortem and forensic evidence, the prosecution presented a foolproof case.

The Fast Track Court pronounced the death penalty on the accused under section 376, 302 and 394 read with 397 of the Indian Penal Code, a decision that was later upheld by the High Court of Kerala. However, on an appeal by the defendant, the Apex Court commuted the death sentence to seven years imprisonment for murder and life imprisonment for rape charges. What led the Apex Court to commute the death penalty was the testimony of two prosecution witnesses. These two witnesses were travelling in the train in a compartment adjacent to the victim's. They testified that on hearing the shrieks of a woman in the ladies' compartment, they tried to stop the train by pulling the chain, but ultimately did not do so because "a middle-aged man in the same compartment told them that the victim herself jumped off from the train and escaped." The Apex Court found that this testimony "militated against the findings of the Trial Court and the High Court that the accused had pushed the victim out of the compartment, after hitting her head against the compartment." Thus, it was not clear whether the accused pushed her or she herself jumped out of the train, and therefore liability could not be attributed to the accused for the injuries sustained due to the fall. Naturally, the accused was awarded the benefit of the doubt. The pertinent point here is that the introduction of two witnesses, instead of augmenting the prosecution's evidence, had weakened the entire case, even though their testimony was based on the words of an unidentified third party. The moral of this case is that the machine of prosecution evidence should not be overloaded or clogged with clumsy witnesses or hearsay.

4

Interrogation
Signs from Body and Mind

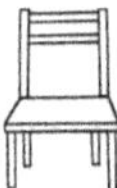

INTERROGATION, IN MANY RESPECTS, is a battle between the mind of the interrogator and that of the accused. This type of conflict creates strong ripples in the mind and body of the accused, which appear as verbal and non-verbal responses. Almost all models and techniques of interrogation attach considerable importance to the proper identification and interpretation of these signs or responses, as they are linked to the success of the interrogation.

From time immemorial, philosophers, researchers and psychoanalysts have studied the interrelationships between mind and body. The Oriental school of thought interpreted such relations based on the *Vedas, Upanishads* and writings of the rishis. The Samkhya school[26] of the Hindu tradition, founded by Kapila, the legendary figure of seventh century BC, attributed three functions to the mind—buddhi or intellect, ahamkara or ego and manas or mentation. Besides these three components, Patanjali, the ancient yogic scholar of second or fourth century BC, found citta or consciousness as the major form of the mind. Citta, as defined by Swami Vivekananda, is the tool through which people perceive the external world. The ego is the self-centred quality whereas buddhi is the ability to distinguish and experience objects through pre-reflective and pre-subjective capabilities. The manas serves as an intermediary between the intellect and the senses. It organizes sensory impressions of objects and integrates them into a temporal framework created by memories and expectations. The intellect experiences them and stimulates signals or responses. The vibrations so created in one's mind appear as verbal and non-verbal responses. This is a continuous process. That is why Yogi Vasishtha[27] stated that the "mind is as fickle as the monkey." By closely observing such gestures and the body language of a person under stress or strain, one can infer what is going on inside that person.

Swami Vivekananda explained the mind-body relationship based on his transcendental experience as, "the body is just the external crust of the mind. They are not two different things, they are just as the oyster and its shell, they are but two aspects of the one thing, the internal substance of oyster takes up matter from outside and manufactures the shell. We shall find how intimately the mind is connected with body. When the mind is disturbed, the body also becomes disturbed."[28] Vishnu Sharma, the legendary Indian scholar of the Gupta era and the author of *Panchatantra*[29] highlighted that intelligent law enforcement personnel can easily identify the guilty and the innocent by properly deciphering their body language; he wrote, "The guilty man is terrified, By reason of his crime, His pride is gone, His powers of speaking fail; His glances rove, his face is pale, The sweat appears on his brow; He stumbles on, he knows not how; His face is pale, all he utters much distorted, for he stutters; The culprit always may be found; To shake and gaze upon the ground; Observe the signs as best you can, And shrewdly pick the guilty man; The innocent is self-reliant; His speech is clear, his glance defiant; His countenance calm & free; His indignation makes his plea".

Significantly, philosophers and psychoanalysts of the West had established similar concepts on the mind-body relationship and its relevance to criminology. Sigmund Freud, the famous Austrian psychoanalyst, made significant contributions in this field. Comparing the human mind to an iceberg, he held that the tip of the iceberg actually visible above the water represented only a tiny portion of the mind, while the huge expanse of ice hidden underneath the water represented the much larger unconscious. He identified three major components of the "unconscious expanse of mind," the id, the ego and the super-ego, with distinct functions. The id represents primitive untamed desire or urges; the ego, the reality and principle of reason, logic and safety; and the super ego, the moral component of personality. The ego's role as a mediator between the id and the super-ego often results in stress, whose signs appear in verbal responses as well as in the body language. Simultaneously, the ego tries to use a variety of means to handle its stress in the form of defence mechanisms (DMs). Sigmund's daughter Anna Freud[30] had generalized the concept of DMs and established that they were key components in the personality of every individual. Proper identification of DMs adopted by the accused during interrogation, and their neutralization by the interrogators using the right techniques are essential for the success of any interrogation. We will discuss DMs and counter-strategies in detail under the Chapter 8.

The modern concept of the human mind also highlights the interrelationship of the mind and body and its relevance in criminal investigations. Just like the four components of the mind as enshrined in Oriental thought, modern psychoanalysts attribute four different roles to the mind—acquire, process, store and retrieve. According to them, perceiving, storing, and retrieving information are active mental processes. They rejected the idea that the human mind functions like a video recorder, automatically recording all experiences exactly as they happen and storing them in an archive until they need to be retrieved. Instead, they found that the mind selectively attends to certain experiences while filtering out others, and is constantly engaged in interpreting their possible meanings and interrelationships. This process results in three modes of memories: Sensory Memory (SM), in which stimuli are only momentarily registered to facilitate perception; Short-Term Memory (STM) or "working memory," which holds information while it is being processed; and Long-Term Memory (LTM), which may be permanent or temporary depending upon various other factors. Such unique features of the human mind and of memory have been used in a number of scientific aids such as the polygraph and brain-mapping. Moreover, by inducing mental states like stress, fatigue and distraction, which affect the mind's capacity to perceive and retrieve memories, interrogators are able to elicit accurate inputs from the interviewee. For this, they cause their suspects physical discomfort, sleep deprivation, sensory deprivation and more. The psychological and emotional effects of such techniques not only help to generate useful information but also diminish resistance, especially by recalcitrant suspects, for example, sleep deprivation has negative effects such as diminished concentration, impairment in cognitive functions and increased suggestibility, which mentally and physically weaken even the hardened suspect. Same is the case with sensory deprivation, which heightens hypnotic susceptibility and cognitive disorganization.

The use of such techniques has evoked serious debate on human behaviour manipulation or brainwashing of suspects during interrogation. These issues came forward following the reported confession of detained US soldiers that the US had dropped bombs filled with germs on a civilian population during the Korean war.[31] There was also speculation that the Soviets and the Chinese had developed scientific mind-control technologies for interrogation. Subsequently, in the 1950s and 1960s, the Central Intelligence Agency (CIA) of the US sponsored a number of research projects to explore how drugs and narcotic substances could be used for sensory deprivation and hypnosis as a part of interrogation techniques. Some of their findings were used in the development of the KUBARK Counterintelligence Interrogation Manual of 1963, which was formally published in the late 1990s. Such research projects laid the foundation for Narco tests, now in use for interrogation in many countries.

Natural or artificially induced stress causes psycho-physical changes that, in turn, manifest as external cues, broadly termed as body language. "Fie, fie upon her! There's language in her eye, her cheek, her lip. Nay, her foot speaks; her wanton spirits look out at every joint and motive of her body."[32] William Shakespeare's description of a character is one of many epic passages that explains the complexity of body language. During interrogation, accused persons demonstrate different postures, movements, expressions, tones, statements and visual cues to conceal their offense or mislead interrogators. Only by properly deciphering these responses can interrogators arrive at right conclusion about the truthfulness or otherwise of their disclosures, based on which they can use other tactics during the interrogation.

More than verbal communication, non-verbal responses are the outward expressions of an individual's feelings, emotions and thoughts. They can be deciphered to reach accurate conclusions on the individual's attitude or approach towards interrogators. Generally hardened criminals or trained agents exercise decisive control over what they say or how they talk. As their verbal responses are thus crafted, it is difficult to assess them as deceptive or true. On the other hand, non-verbal responses are more likely to fall outside a subject's full awareness and may provide a better source of cues for detecting deception. Facial expressions are considered to be the most prominent cue. Over a century and a half ago, Charles Darwin[33] conducted pioneering research in this area and his famous work, *The Expressions of the Emotions in Man and Animals*,[34] established the link between facial expressions and emotions.

Most modern researchers like Desmond Morris, Paul Ekman and Wallace Friesen have endorsed Darwin's findings. Morris suggested that there were a number of expressions and gestures "that constantly communicated the same message across cultural and linguistic boundaries."[35] He found that bodily activities were the unconscious behaviours of the conscious and unconscious mind, which thus revealed their feelings and expressions rather than articulating them through conscious words. Ekman's famous quote, "Anger may leak out through a clenched fist or in a tensed posture,"[36] exemplified the importance of the clinical implications of human body language. Further, he held that the emotions of anger, disgust, fear, happiness, sadness and surprise have generated a more specific set of facial expressions as compared to contempt, embarrassment, interest, pain and shame, which were expressed in lesser degrees. He claimed that these emotions are universally generated and recognized across all cultures. Moreover, in 1978, Ekman and Friesen developed the Facial Action Coding System (FACS)[37] to measure all visible facial muscle movements including the head and eye movements.

Researchers continued their efforts to quantify facial expressions in different scenarios. In 2001, two separate research teams consisting of members from Carnegie Mellon University,[38] the University of Pittsburgh and the University of California (San Diego), and the Salk Institute[39] developed a non-intrusive automatic facial expression recognition system after quantitatively analyzing spontaneous facial expressions of many samples in different situations. The Auction Units (AUs) independently developed by them were of immense practical application in deciphering the facial expressions of criminals and suspected persons. These efforts to give scientific orientation to the analysis of facial expressions have gained further momentum as researchers had developed real-time, fully automated systems to recognize facial expressions. One of the major landmarks[40] in this effort was the classification of facial expressions on the basis of specific emotions, namely happiness, sadness, surprise, disgust, fear, anger and neutral. This classification is perhaps akin to the Navarasa or the nine unique emotional expressions of Indian classics, which are: shringara (love/beauty), hasya (laughter or humour), karuna (empathy or sorrow), raudra (anger), veera (courage), bhayanaka (terror or fear), bibhatsa (disgust), adbutha (surprise or wonder) and santha (peace or tranquillity). Through proper interpretation of such emotional expressions, experienced interrogators can draw vital conclusions on the attitude of an accused and on the truthfulness or falsity of their disclosures during interrogation.

Eye responses are one of the most visible forms of facial expression. Researchers have established that some eye movement features are useful for detecting lies. In its simplest version, eye contact normally determines whether a person is interested in a conversation. When a suspect stares uneasily at the interrogators, it might indicate fear or intimidation. A direct stare is normally associated with aggression or a challenging stance. Many other features such as pupil dilation, eye blinks, saccades and fixations are helpful in ascertaining the veracity of a suspect's statements. Frequent blinking usually indicates nervousness or deception. A saccade, which is a rapid, intermittent eye movement that occurs when the eyes look quickly from one thing to another, is yet another useful expression to detect lies and truth. There are many other gestures and postures that indicate truth or lies. Frequent movements of the legs, feet, head and trunk, shifting body positions and covering gestures such as placing a hand over the mouth while talking, ear tugging and the like are effective cues for deception.

Paralinguistic cues such as voice pitch, speed and breathing, pronunciation, articulation, pauses and punctuation shed a lot of light on the mental framework of the person under interrogation and the veracity of his or her disclosures. During interrogation, a suspect's voice projects a mosaic of emotions such as tension, fear, dislike of certain topics and confusion. Skilled interrogators closely monitor such responses and draw major conclusions. Mechanisms such as Computer Voice Stress Analysis (CVSA) have been developed to interpret such variations and arrive at conclusions. Researchers have also attempted to develop methods for systematically evaluating verbal responses. Statement Validity

Assessment (SVA) and Reality Monitoring are the two major approaches. SVA involves the use of criteria-based content analysis that attempts to provide some common methodology for evaluating the content of verbal communication. Reality Monitoring attempts to determine the validity of statements by assessing the clarity and realism of a narrative along with contextual information that indicates the presence or absence of details that link elements of time, space and sensory perceptions with the primary content of that narrative.

The process of accurately reading the body language, verbal and non-verbal, of an accused is a difficult task, for which interrogators require proper skills and experience. The critical first step is to establish the baseline character of the accused through the non-accusatory interview. Just as people show individual variations in various physiological or metabolic features such as blood pressure, pulse rate, etc., people similarly exhibit different verbal and non-verbal responses under pressure or stress. Regional, cultural, familial factors, or overall personality can significantly influence a person's behaviour and body language in such situations. While comparing the baseline character of the accused with his or her verbal and non-verbal responses during interrogation, interrogators need to consider such factors to properly decipher these symbols and arrive at correct conclusions. Based on the experience gathered during interrogation assignments and authentic research by psychologists and experts, some of these common body language indicators that help to identify the innocent and the guilty are catalogued for ready reference. However, the fundamental principle stands that no suspect or accused should be branded as truthful or deceptive exclusively based on body language features.

Table III: Body Language and Non-verbal Indicators and their Inferences

Response or Body Language	Inference
Clumsy and uncoordinated walk to the IR room, arms are close to sides	To appear smaller and less important
Walks close to the wall with shorter steps	Consciously avoiding others
One shoulder up, right hand inside pocket	Determined to face the situation
Buttoning up and adjusting clothing	Determined to face interrogators
Head remains stationary, but eyes move	Indication of fear or guilt
Continually yawns	Very high state of fight or flight
Fixed facial expression for more than 10 seconds during first interaction	Display of false emotion and hiding something
Relocating chair or moving front table to front side	Indication of guilt or likely to begin lying
Sitting with legs spread, or leaning forward or hands on thighs, or thumbs pointing towards each other and elbows pointing outward	Aggressive and non-cooperative
Sitting with legs apart, leaning forward with forearms resting on thighs or sitting with legs crossed over the knees	Characteristics of a subject who has been in jail or a criminal
Sitting still, arms crossed, non-emotional facial expressions (silence ploy)	Manipulative effort of a guilty suspect

Right hand under the table, left armpit or left hand, or sliding into a pocket	Stress and deception
Rocks backward and begins to squirm or move	Subject begins to be deceptive
Presents diary, phone records, affidavits, tape recordings, religious books or brings up health issues or family connections	Guilty and manipulative efforts
White of the eye above the irises of both eyes	Indicates great anger
White below the irises	Spiritual distress and depression
Anger against interrogator or against issues and facts presented	Indication of a deceptive suspect
Claims to be entitled to special treatment	Clear manipulative move
Dry mouth, licking of lips, swallowing, clearing throat or making odd noises	High stress and fear. May be indication of guilt
Scratching the top of the head	Suggests confusion
Pulls down sides of mouth by fingers	Stress and difficulty with the questions
Rubbing above the top lip below the nose	Doubts about questions
Rubbing chin while smiling slightly	Indication for admission/ confession
Touching area around forehead with the fingers of one hand, or running fingertips up and down vertically	Trying to make up mind whether to say or not say something
Placing hands over the mouth or fingers touching the bottom of nose	Rejecting the interrogator and blocking out the flow of information

Rubbing the area below the right eye	Deceptive effort
Pressing a fist firmly below his chin	Reflects anger
Rubbing the inner corner of either eye	Indication of fatigue of the suspect
Pulling either cheek and knuckles or fingers	Feeling of great insecurity
Slower inhalation in response to a question	To buy time for answering
Deep breath or excessive inhale or exhale	Indication of depression and stress
Long extended sigh at the end of an answer	Relief and indication to give up or has given up
Deeper and longer breath and expanded chest	Great stress and deception
Breaks eye contact	Probable lying
Pupils fully dilated	Emotional or indication of lying
Stops blinking and begins staring	Totally focused on the question
Rapid blinking	Nervous or probably lying
Closed eyes	Emotional escape or probably lying
Pitched voice—high or low	Deception or probably guilty
Breakers such as quivering or stammering	Probably guilty or indication of stress
Special vocal expressions or crying or laughing	Emotional or probably guilty or indication of remorse
Space fillers such as "Oh," "Ah," etc.	Deception or probably guilty

Table IV: Verbal Indicators and Phrases and their Inferences

Verbal Response	Indication
Final queries such as "Is that everything?"	Indication that there is more to reveal
Blurring words (around, about, assume)	To throw the interrogator off
Retractions (however, nor, yet, neither)	Hiding evidence of involvement
Movement words (went, resumed, proceed)	Withholding or deceiving
Verbatim reporting or narration	Truthful or reliable
A hedge (pretty sure, really, perhaps)	Not truthful or deceptive
Uncertainty (I believe, I think, I guess)	Concealing facts or truth
Indirect, roundabout replies ("Tom, are you involved in this theft?" Answer: "No, sir. I think someone who steals is bad and they should be punished.")	To create distance from any real, personal or emotional involvement
Avoid answering a question directly ("Did you steal the money? Answer: "Where did you hear that one?")	Deceptive, defensive strategy
Replies not relevant to the question ("Did you steal the money?" Answer: "I am a good mother.")	Effort to direct the interrogation to suspect's favour
Linking truth and lies ("I admit that I know the girl, I admit that we went to the movie on that night, but I didn't misbehave with her.")	Deceptive and manipulative tactics by using a convincing alibi or pleas

5

Interrogation
Constitution and Laws

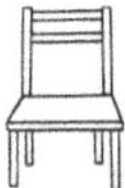

INTERROGATION OF AN ACCUSED or a suspect is a complex but challenging task, which must be accomplished within the bounds of the law. Several constitutional and legal parameters have been put into place to ensure the rights and privileges of the accused and to streamline the functioning of agencies involved in such tasks. The origin of many of these provisions like Presumption of Innocence can be traced back to the golden period of the Greek civilization. The well-known and widely accepted legal maxim which holds that "it is better to allow one hundred guilty to escape, lest one innocent is unjustly punished" was evident in the laws of Sparta and Athens. The concept's source can be established from the writings of Trajan to Julius Frontinus[41] commanding that "no man should be condemned on a criminal charge in his absence, because it was better to let the crime of a guilty person go unpunished than to condemn the innocent."[42] Subsequently, many such concepts have become the cornerstone of criminal jurisprudence.

The Right against Self-incrimination and similar provisions, which are incorporated in the constitution of almost all countries, ensure the right of a person to refuse to answer questions or otherwise give testimony against himself or herself—testimony that will incriminate the person. Professor Mark Godsey of the University of Cincinnati Law has said that, "the self-incrimination clause is undoubtedly the most appropriate provision in the Constitution with which to directly regulate confessions because it unambiguously speaks to the issue by banning the use of compulsion to obtain self-incriminating statements that are later admitted at trial against the suspect." [43] The concept existed in England much earlier than the sixteenth century but it came into the sharp focus in the immediate aftermath of Star Chamber practices, which prescribed that persons charged by tribunals were forced to take an ex-officio oath by which they were bound to provide truthful answer(s) to all the questions that were to be put to them. With the abolition of the Star Chamber practices, it was recognized that no man is bound to incriminate himself on any charge against him or before any court. In England, the practice of judicial questioning of accused persons at trial continued till the eighteenth century. The Universal Declaration of Human Rights[44] during the twentieth century gave increased global acceptance to this right, which found due place in criminal law and in the dispensation of justice.

The United States, an inheritor of common law traditions and ideals had upheld the rights and privileges of persons even before the American revolution or war of independence. The

Fifth Amendment of the US constitution, as well as provisions in many state constitutions and laws, prohibits the government from requiring a person to be a witness against himself or to furnish evidence against himself. This right under the Fifth Amendment, often called 'pleading the Fifth,'[45] is now applicable to the states through the due process clause of the Fourteenth Amendment and is applicable in any situation, civil or criminal, where the state attempts to compel incriminating testimony. This protective clause of the right against self-incrimination not only covers the accused but also the witnesses.

The Right against Self-incrimination or Right to Silence, as enshrined in the Fifth Amendment, came under thorough review of the US Supreme Court in the case of Miranda v. Arizona.[46] In this case, Ernesto Miranda, a Mexican immigrant living in Arizona was arrested and interrogated for kidnapping and raping a woman. During a two-hour long interrogation, Miranda confessed to the crime. However, the police had not advised Miranda on his constitutional right for engaging an attorney nor against self-incrimination. Nonetheless, he signed a written confession. The Trial Court convicted him for the offense. The Supreme Court of Arizona reconfirmed the lower court's decision, holding that procuring the confession without the presence of a lawyer had not violated Miranda's constitutional rights. On an appeal, the US Supreme Court, which ruled on the case along with four other cases with similar contentions, reversed the Arizona SC's decision on the grounds that presenting Miranda's confession as evidence violated his constitutional rights under the Fifth and Sixth Amendments. The Court held that there can be no doubt that the Fifth Amendment privilege is available outside of criminal court proceedings and serves to protect persons in all settings in which their freedom of action is curtailed in any significant way and in which they might be compelled to incriminate themselves. Accordingly, the Supreme Court issued specific guidelines that the accused should be warned prior to any interrogation that he has the right to remain silent, that anything that he says can be used against him in a court of law, that he has the right to the presence of an attorney and that if he cannot afford an attorney, one will be appointed to him prior to the questioning, if he so desires. These guidelines for the police and investigators during interrogation are known as Miranda warnings.

Jurists and criminologists are divided on the Miranda clause pertaining to the Right to Counsel of an accused. In Watts v. Indiana,[47] Justice Jackson decreed that exposing a suspect "without counsel to questioning which may and is intended to convict him, is a real peril to individual freedom" and that it "largely negates the benefits of the constitutional guarantee of the right to assistance of counsel." But at the same time, he cautioned that allowing a suspect access to counsel "means a real peril to solution of the crime." On the other hand, Justice Frankfurter, another judge on the same bench, saw a contradiction between access to a lawyer and police interrogation. He found that interrogation was permissible and required reasonable means to make questioning effective. "Legal counsel for the suspect will generally prove a thorough obstruction to the investigation. Indeed, even to inform the suspect of his legal right to keep silent will prove an obstruction." In so far as the prevailing practice in India is concerned, the Apex Court in Nandini Sapthathy v. PL Dani and others[48] made a commendatory suggestion that investigating agencies like the police can use their discretion in deciding the presence of a counsel to assist the accused during his cross-examination or questioning while in custody. Significantly, the Court did not make it mandatory, nor a strict legal obligation on the part of police or other agencies during the interrogation of accused.

Similarly critical were the Executive wing and the law-enforcers, as many felt that it was unfair to inform suspected criminals of their rights. Former US President Richard Nixon and the US conservatives denounced Miranda for undermining the efficiency of the police and feared that the provisions would lead to an increase in crime. Nixon, as President, promised to appoint judges who would critically review the Miranda provisions. Subsequently, the US Supreme Court, through a number of judgments, disagreed with certain Miranda clauses. For example, in Raffel v. US, the Court held that at the very moment a suspect cooperates and answers questions and consents to a search, the suspect gives up those rights and must continue that cooperation and consent through to that person's possible or eventual arrest, trial and judgment. Similarly, in Berghuis v. Thompkins,[49] the Court found that "a suspect's ambiguous or equivocal statement or lack of statements does not mean that police should end an interrogation." In his dissenting order, Justice Sotomayor described the majority's decision as, "a substantial retreat from the protection against compelled self-incrimination that Miranda v. Arizona has long provided during custodial interrogation."

A majority of the countries in the world, especially those committed to democracy and rule of law, have woven the Miranda rulings or Right to Silence as a constitutional guarantee. Nations that have not fully upheld the provisions have included appropriate articles in their constitution or framed rules in line with the spirit of those rights. For example, in Australia, an accused or a suspect charged under the State and Federal Crimes

Act is given the protection of a right to refuse to answer questions by lawmen during the process of police enquiry. The Right to Silence is protected under Section 7 and Section 11(c) of the Canadian Charter of Rights and Freedoms. The accused may not be compelled to function as a witness against himself in criminal proceedings and therefore only voluntary statements made to police are admissible as evidence.

Similar provisions are enshrined in the Indian Constitution and criminal laws. For example, Right to Silence is a fundamental right guaranteed under Article 20(3) of the Constitution, which says that "no person accused of any offence shall be compelled to be a witness against himself." This privilege is fundamental to Common law and criminal jurisprudence and has its equivalent in the Magna Carta[50] or the Talmud[51] or the Miranda clause. Article 20(3) is often referred to as the article on the right of an accused against self-incrimination. From a legal point of view, this article contains three major components: a) the right available to any person accused of an offense, b) protection against any compulsion to such person to be a witness and c) protection against such compulsion in his giving evidence against himself. Legally, in order to claim the protection under Article 20(3), all these components should co-exist.

The protection under Article 20(3) in criminal, civil and other offenses has come under the scrutiny of the Apex Court and various other courts. According to the Supreme Court, this protection extends to "juristic persons"[52] but may not extend to cases where the accused is being interrogated in an investigation under a law like the Customs Act or a law involving a civil violation because the protection of the law is intended only in criminal cases.[53] The expression "accused of an offense" and the use of the word "compelled" in the Article has been extensively discussed by various High Courts and the Apex Court. The Supreme Court, jettisoning its earlier restrictive views of the expression "accused of an offense," clarified that it included not only a person formally brought into the police diary but also covers a suspect, who can both claim the protection under the Article 20(3) (Nandini Satpathy v. P.L. Dani and others). The Court held that the dictates of Article 20(3) as well as the emphatic proscriptions of Section 161(2) of the Criminal Procedure Code, 1973, giving protection to an accused not to answer questions of an investigator that would expose that accused to a criminal charge, penalty or forfeiture, run in tandem and are virtually the same. Similarly, the use of the word "compelled" is of immense significance because the act of "compulsion" is the most vital and essential ingredient of the article. Thus, if an accused confesses without any form of threat, inducement or promise, such a confession cannot be construed as having been obtained under "compulsion," though subsequently, the person may retract the said confession.[54] Similarly, the provisions of Article 20(3) do not bar an accused from voluntarily agreeing to be examined as a witness.

Arrest or custody of the accused is a pre-condition for a successful interrogation. Thus, for an arrest, there are also protective clauses and procedures. Article 22(1) ensures that no person who is arrested shall be detained in custody without being informed of the grounds for such arrest, nor shall the person be denied the right to consult, and to be defended by, a legal practitioner of his choice. For the protective provisions of an arrested person, the Constitution provides Section 50(1)[55] and 303 of CrPc.[56] In DK Basu v. State of West Bengal (1997),[57] the Apex Court laid down guidelines to be followed by the police while arresting a person. These guidelines include: a) proper recording of the particulars of the police personnel who arrest or interrogate the person; b) preparation of an arrest memo with the time and date of arrest attested by witness and countersigned by the arrestee; c) intimation of arrest to a person known to the arrestee as soon as possible; d) notification of arrest through a legal aid organization within 8-10 hours after the arrest; e) informing the arrestee about his right to have someone informed of his arrest; f) proper entry in the diary of the police station of detention with the details, like the person informed and name and particulars of police personnel in whose custody the arrestee is; g) medical examination of the arrestee and proper recording of grievous and minor injuries on his body and h) forwarding copies of all documents of arrest to the *Ilaqua* Magistrate.

The Indian Evidence Act, 1872 contains crucial provisions ensuring the rights of the accused or suspects during investigations or interrogations. Sections 24 to 27 of the Act cover these aspects. Section 24 underlines that a confession made by an accused person is irrelevant in a criminal proceeding if the confession appears to the Court to have been caused by any inducement, threat or promise. Similarly, Section 25 holds that no confession made to a police officer shall be proved as against a person accused of any offence. Section 26 maintains that no confession made by any person while he is in the custody of a police officer shall be proved as against such person, unless it is made in the immediate presence of a Magistrate. Section 164 of the Cr Pc specifies how confessional statements should be recorded. Only those statements recorded in accordance with the law have evidentiary value. Section 27 provides that a confessional statement made to a police officer or while an accused is in police custody can be proved against him if the same leads to the discovery of an unknown fact. This section assumes considerable significance in interrogation and gathering of evidence. It stipulates that the discoveries or recoveries made by the investigators on the basis of the revelations made by an accused will be admissible as evidence.

The basic objective of these sections in The Indian Evidence Act is to prevent practices of torture or other unlawful actions by law enforcement officers in extracting confessions from the accused persons. There has been a lot of debate on the question of the admissibility as evidence of the confession made by an accused before the police. Quoting existing practices in many western countries like the UK and US, some law enforcement officers and jurists argue for such changes in our criminal justice system. Those who oppose such reforms highlight that the police and other investigation agencies in India have yet to rise to the level of the forces in those countries in matters of professionalism, integrity and uprightness. As such, granting such legal powers to these agencies would adversely affect the functioning of our criminal justice system.

Such issues need to be considered in relation to the concept of 'due process of law' that essentially emphasizes the need for the police and other agencies to demonstrate due diligence in all the laws and all legal proceedings while dealing with the accused. This term, which was first employed way back in 1354 in a statute of Edward II, has found expression in the Fifth Amendment of the US Constitution, which has become a part of the basic guiding principles of all legal processes in the US. Notions of due process were slowly added in the legal texts of other countries, especially after World War II. For example, the US Constitution guarantees that the government cannot take away a person's basic rights to "life, liberty or property, without due process of law." In India, the term 'due process' does not find a place in the relevant text of the Constitution, instead the phrase "procedure established by law" figures in it.

As per the due process norms, confessions during interrogation are constitutional and thus admissible in criminal proceedings, provided they are voluntary. However, there are many problems associated with the voluntariness test. As the main task of the police, detectives or investigators is to obtain incriminating evidence during the interrogation of suspects, there is general tendency to obtain confessions at any cost, even resorting torture and other inhuman methods. Most illustrative examples are the 1989 Central Park Jogger case of New York City and the Stephanie Crowe murder case[58] of Escondido, California in 1998. In the Central Park rape case, five juveniles who didn't commit the crime were tried for various offenses and convicted on their confessions and each spent between 7 and 13 years in prison. Years later, a serial rapist admitted that he alone was responsible for the rape. Similarly, the now proven to be false confession of three juveniles, suspected to be involved in the murder of 13-year-old Stephanie Crowe evoked widespread public debate and awareness on problematic police interrogation techniques leading to false confessions and miscarriage of justice. In this case too, the real killer was Richard Tuite, a vagabond in the area. Wickersham[59] has underscored that there is always a danger that the process of interrogation may develop into the third degree. Once the interrogation has begun, the police or other officials are naturally reluctant to leave off until the desired information has been obtained, regardless of the suspect's fatigue or need for sleep. In William Sargent's words, "The stress that the interrogators put the subject through causes distinct and predictable physiological effects that result in the subject losing his or her previous sets of beliefs."[60] This change in beliefs ultimately leads to confession that is not voluntary or admissible as evidence in criminal cases.

Of course, there is a lack of international consensus on the issue of torture and other human rights violations during investigations of organized crimes such as terrorism. Considering the changing geo-political scenario, it is too soon to predict if the pendulum will swing back toward an increased acceptance of torture in interrogations. The threat of terrorism and the fight against global terrorism very often leads to the violation of constitutional and legal provisions ensuring the rights and privileges of the accused during interrogation. Instead, inhumane methods of interrogation have been adopted against the detained suspected terrorists as the world witnessed in Guantanamo Bay and other similar interrogation camps after the 9/11 terror attacks in the US.

6

Planning, Preparation and Settings in Interrogation

ANY INTERROGATION IS AN interaction between two individuals, the interrogator and the suspect, in which both of them are unable to anticipate the nuances, challenges and turns of events during the interaction, nor the final outcome. Nonetheless, exhaustive planning and preparation enable an interrogator or interrogation team to attain some understanding of the issues that are likely to surface during the interrogation. This allows them to work out a suitable strategy or tactics to deal with an array of possible tangents or diversions and to devise an acceptable alternative case of intractable defiance by the interrogatee. Significantly, a properly framed interrogation approach, plan and questioning methodology will progress logically towards a predefined objective. But achieving the objective requires an exquisitely detailed, yet highly accommodative map of the course to follow from the start of the interrogation.

For the preparation of a detailed action plan, the interrogators should be acquainted with the case or incident and the suspect's background. This should include the time and conditions of arrest, place(s) and duration of confinement, recoveries made during the time of arrest or during search of hideouts or premises. Ali Soufan[61] of the FBI, one of the most successful interrogators of al-Qaeda, explains how meticulously he and his team extensively prepared for the interrogation of al-Qaeda operatives. They had collected everything about the outfit from intelligence records and agents—their main areas of operation, pseudonyms of important leaders, places visited and contacts established, inputs on the interaction of the interrogatee (al-Qaeda) with other leaders, and more. Such basic preparation signals to the detainee that the interrogators knew all about him and any lie will be easily uncovered. Moreover, by preparing for different hypothetical situations, the interrogators can reasonably predict what the suspect might say and where the evidence could lead, thereby lessening the chances of the suspect taking them by surprise.

Thus, the investigators should try to collect as many details about the suspects as possible during the preparation stage. These include their present physical and mental condition, home environment, social attitudes, hobbies, any deviant behaviour such as addictions to drugs, alcohol or gambling, religious or fundamentalist ideologies or prejudices, motive or opportunities to commit the offense and approach towards investigators. Normally, these details are collected through a pre-interrogation interview. The Reid technique holds that conducting an interview before the start of the interrogation not only helps to establish rapport and trust with the suspect but also enables the interrogators to learn information about the suspect that will help in conducting the interrogation. According to Reid, this interview should be non-accusatory and designed to elicit information about the offense itself, the suspect or suspects and the victims.

Very often, the first challenge interrogators face is collecting details of suspects whose background is unknown or shrouded in secrecy. In such cases, investigators need to conduct general research. Assume that the detained suspect is an infiltrator from the Punjab province of Pakistan. The interrogator must obtain a detailed background of the region, with particular reference to the Partition of India in 1947 and the formation of Pakistan, and how the Punjab province has unique demographic and cultural similarities with many parts of India. In the wake of past conflicts between the two countries and continued hostile relations, there are organized moves from the Pakistan side to infiltrate into India for various clandestine operations. That being the general historical background of the suspect, the interrogator may then proceed to other general sources for more relevant inputs. They should probe into prior interrogation reports of suspects who were detained under similar situations. They should also access collaborative tools such as existing databases on hostile outfits operating from the region, prominent leaders, their linkages and modus operandi of operations. Based on the suspect's background and profile, the interrogators should plan suitable interrogation strategies or approaches and frame initial questions to elicit critical intelligence. Usually, during the interrogation of hostile elements or terrorists, the interrogation plan should invariably focus on four critical areas: organizational set-up of the hostile outfit, present situation, mission or tasks assigned and execution.

The conditions and arrangement of the interrogation room assume considerable importance here. The interrogation room should be set up in such a manner to ensure a sense of privacy for the suspect. This is based on the psychological premise that human beings are more comfortable revealing secrets in privacy. Equally important is the removal of police paraphernalia from both the room and the interrogator's person. An ideal interrogation room should be a small, controlled and sound insulated one, without any distractions like a window, telephone, clock or intercom. The lighting should be adequate but not excessive or glaring, so that the suspect's natural facial expressions can be easily read. Similarly, the noise level should be as low as possible so that even the low-pitched responses from the suspect are clearly audible. Chairs should be arranged so that the interrogator and the suspect are separated by about four to five feet and should face each other without any other object or obstruction between them. In a nutshell, the elimination of a formal police atmosphere combined with the illusion of remoteness and privacy and the lack of sound can have a sudden, devastating effect upon the suspect's composure which can be advantageous for the interrogators to elicit responses from the suspect.

A few experts like Aubry[62] suggest that there must be a reception room adjoining the interrogation room with a two-way buzzer communication system between the two rooms. The question of such facilities arises when the interrogatee is provided with legal or medical assistance, as directed by judicial bodies. The legal or medical experts can use these facilities in order to meet any exigencies, however, it should be ensured that their presence in no way hampers the interrogation, nor does it deter the suspect from cooperating with the interrogators. Another suggestion pertains to the use of a one-way mirror and a concealed microphone so that observers can monitor the interrogation while maintaining the necessary privacy. Such an arrangement can facilitate the fellow interrogators to prepare themselves for subsequent sessions of interrogation—they can prepare by observing the suspect's behaviour and deciphering verbal and non-verbal responses. This can also protect the interrogators from allegations of misconduct or excesses, and help them continue observing the suspect when he is left alone in the interrogation room.

With the advancements and developments in cyberspace, such conventional monitoring mechanisms have been replaced by new technologies. Modern interrogation rooms of various law enforcement and investigation agencies have open or surreptitious video-recording facilities to monitor interrogations, especially in sensitive cases. Countries like the US, UK and Australia have legally enforced videotaping of interrogations. The American Bar Association's Criminal Justice Section and the New York County Lawyers Association argue that the practice of videotaping in interrogations should be mandated in all states and federal jurisdictions. Concerns about false confessions frame their argument. Similarly, the National Association of Criminal Defence Lawyers supports the practice as "a simple procedure that would deter human rights violations, reduce the risk of wrongful convictions due to false confessions, and greatly enhance the truth-seeking process by resolving factual disputes concerning interrogation." No doubt, surreptitious videotaping has many advantages. There has been general consensus among criminologists and investigators that videotaping needs to be done surreptitiously in order to ensure better results in interrogations. Reid and Inbau, the authors of the Reid model of interrogation, held that guilty suspects were less likely to tell the truth and/or confess if they were being electronically recorded because they would be "over-concerned" that their disclosures would become incriminating evidence or intelligence. They substantiated their claims via a study in Alaska and Minnesota, which revealed that when the video-recording device was never visible, interrogators obtained an 82% confession rate as against a 43% rate when the device was visible. Aubry,[63] who endorsed the need for hidden recording devices, argued that a recording "should definitely be made of the entire interrogation procedure, if for no other reason than to demonstrate conclusively that the confession was secured in conformity with legal safeguards." He argued that such measures may help reduce doubts as to the trustworthiness or voluntariness of the confession and enhance the confession's evidentiary value during the trial.

When it comes to preparing interrogation questions in advance, there is no consensus. According to Dillon,[64] questions should be prepared beforehand and written down on paper. In many instances, investigation agencies adopt such practices in the case of high-profile suspects subjected to interrogation or questioning for a brief period—as directed by the court—mainly for economic offenses such as corruption or money laundering. The effectiveness of such methods is disputable. Interrogators with vast experience hold that confronting the suspect with prepared questions inhibits flexibility and retards the process of eliciting useful inputs as the suspects cunningly try to evade such questions by keeping silent or giving inconclusive replies. According to them, the best method is to start thinking of questions in the interrogation room itself, after fully understanding the mood of the suspect.

7

Qualities and Skills of an Interrogator

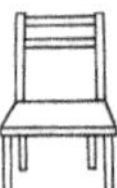

THE ART OF INTERROGATION is a science, a behavioural science, in which the key players are the interrogators. Those who are well-versed in the various nuances of this art agree that not just any one can be a successful interrogator. Those who study and practice this art for years, and possess certain personality traits and skills can excel in this field and make their mark. In the words of Hans Gustav Adolf Gross,[65] the famous Austrian jurist and criminologist, an ideal interrogator is one "who knows men; who is gifted with a good memory and presence of mind; who takes pleasure in his work and zealously abandons himself to it; who is always scrupulously bound by the rules laid down in law and who sees always in the accused a fallen brother or one who wrongfully suspected, he will question well. But an officer who is wanting in a single one of the qualifications will never do any good." Using three German words—Ehr (honour), Lehr (education/knowledge) and Wehr (moral virtue)—Hans Scharff, the leading interrogator of the German Air Force during World War II, highlighted that an ideal interrogator should have knowledge, talent, experience, moral values and maturity.

The commonly accepted interrogation models such as Reid and Kinesic emphasize such qualities or skills as prerequisites for a successful interrogation. Interrogators must be intelligent, with a sound practical understanding of human nature, and have a versatile personality to get along with others, especially persons from different backgrounds. In the words of Stan B Walters, "the best interrogators are those who have learned to observe and interpret human communication behaviour, are introspective enough to know themselves and have developed a broad-based understanding of other personalities."[66] Patience and a high index of suspicion are important attributes, as is an intense interest in the field of interrogation. Good interrogators augment this intense interest with a continual study of behaviour analysis in the fields of psychology and psychopathology, as well as of interrogation techniques. As the interrogator has to play the roles of both interrogator and interviewer, he needs all the characteristics of a good interviewer: a friendly, personable, non-judgmental, unprejudiced and objective manner; a genuine curiosity and concern about other people; the ability to separate the suspect from the crime; comfort in asking questions and the ability to be a good listener. Knowledge of the legal regulations surrounding interrogation is also indispensable. An interrogator should have good memory, determination, the ability to control emotions and a gift of gab with sound communication skills.

"The interrogator must be confident and comfortable in his own skin."[67]

Lieutenant Albert F Pierce, Jr of the Massachusetts Institute of Technology (MIT) Police Department, who worked in different areas of policing for the Massachusetts State Police conducted an empirical study[68] on various policing techniques including interrogation. He found that among the various characteristics of a good interrogator, the most significant ones are "true liking of people, an ability to get along with people of all backgrounds, comfort in talking to people, and knowledge of how to do it." According to him, anyone who wants to be a successful interrogator needs to be a good actor—to convey sympathy, empathy and other emotions that the interrogator does not really feel. To develop such innate skills or abilities is a real challenge facing budding interrogators. Pierce narrated a few personal anecdotes and approaches. As a young detective, he used to sit outside or in bars with his colleagues and have close interactions with people in order to observe their behaviour and pick up people-skills to improve on the basic abilities he already possessed. This also allowed him to gain an understanding of how people act and react in various settings. Equally important is the interrogator's ability to know himself and his limitations. Successful interrogators must know how to restrain their own egos or to wriggle out of any situation or interrogation they cannot handle.

As the popular dictum goes, "know thyself is the beginning of all wisdom." Beyond knowing oneself, a successful interrogator should be able to effectively and accurately assess the interrogatee's emotional and psychological state, veracity and knowledgeability. A proper understanding of the behaviour, approach and emotions of the suspect at the right phase of the interrogation is vital for eliciting truth. Normally, consistent interrogation experience helps develop these assessment skills. However, interrogators must be sufficiently disciplined to avoid drawing unsupported, possibly self-serving conclusions about his or her assessment skills. Such unique and specific qualities of an interrogator, to properly understand himself and the interrogatee, remind us of the observation of the renowned Chinese Military strategist Sun Tzu, "If you know your enemy and know yourself, you need not fear the result of a hundred battles. But, if you know yourself but not the enemy, for every victory gained you will also suffer a defeat."[69] His words are as true in the interrogation room as on the battlefield. In a nutshell, an interrogator acting upon this counsel would be reasonably expected to spend considerable time identifying and deconstructing the interrogatee's resistant posture and strategies.

These intra- and inter-personal abilities play a crucial role in developing interrogation skills. Intra-personal skills include: self-analysis or introspection, adherence to moral and ethical values, a proper appreciation of others' feelings or emotions. Inter-personal abilities like good verbal and non-verbal communication, a capacity to understand the intentions, motivations and desires of other people and flexibility at socializing with others, considerably help interrogators to establish rapport with suspects.

It has been debated how far the "acceptable" inhumane interrogation approach, as demonstrated in the Stanford Prison Experiment,[70] can be used to coerce information. According to one school of thought, such behaviour is justified during the interrogation of terrorists or trained agents. Another school of criminologists and interrogators oppose such behaviour, holding that non-coercive methods are more viable and useful in generating real actionable inputs even in the case of counter-terrorism operations. However, when coercive behaviour or methods go beyond the contours of existing rules and regulations of interrogation, the interrogators come under scrutiny and criticism, as happened in the Abu Gharib Interrogation centre in Iraq or the Guantanamo Bay detention camp in Cuba. While official military and government representatives shifted the blame for such violations onto a few bad apples among interrogators or investigators, certain sections of criminologists and researchers interpreted them as manifestation of the systemic problems of a formally established military incarceration system and interrogation methods of Prisoners of Wars or terror detainees using Enhanced Interrogation Techniques. Zimbardo, the architect of the Stanford Prison Experiment, succinctly described such organizational deviancy as, "I argue that we all have the capacity for love and evil—to be Mother Theresa, to be Hitler or Saddam Hussein. It's the situation that brings that out."[71]

The system that creates and maintains such situations needs to be through institutional or organizational mechanisms in order to contain any Lucifer Effect among interrogators—deviant, aberrant or undesirable behaviour perpetrating evil or resorting to torture. Interrogators should uphold constitutional and legal provisions and fulfil due process, ensuring the rights and privileges of the accused during interrogation. To inculcate such traits, there should be systematic screening and a rigorous selection process for those inducted into interrogation teams or assigned with interrogation tasks. Authors like Aubry[72] hold that at least five years of police experience, with at least two of those spent in bona fide investigative duties of criminal violations, preferably as a detective or plainclothesmen, may be required as basic qualifications for induction. Such field investigation experience and apprenticeship as an interrogator, with continual training and review, as well as education in psychology, physiology, criminology, sociology and basic physical sciences, will help develop personal and professional qualities in the inducted personnel. However, Ali Soufan, one of the leading interrogators of the FBI, who has successfully interrogated dozens of senior al-Qaeda leaders, has a different approach. According to him, "While interrogation techniques are taught at the Academy, being in a classroom is very different from being in an interrogation room and seeing an expert questioner at work. The interrogation skills and knowledge cannot be picked up from a few sessions; they come from studying the group and the subject, and lots of interrogation experience working alongside experts."[73]

Consistent and extensive experience in the field enables interrogators to develop their professional skills and competency. A number of studies on the desirable qualities of an interrogator have established that experience attained through the interrogation of different types of interrogatees enables interrogators to develop core qualities such as an ability to quickly recognize crucial leads and modify their nature of questioning and effective assessment of the personality and motives of the interrogatees. Thus intelligence, law enforcement and security agencies in different countries have constituted specialized interrogation cells or branches whose personnel undergo regular training to enhance their knowledge, skills and other professional traits in line with new challenges that they have to face in their field of operations. Over the years, by interrogating a wide variety of suspects, these personnel develop necessary skills, sound knowledge and strategies and a deep understanding of human psychology and weaknesses that make them the best professional interrogators.

8

Main Models of Interrogation

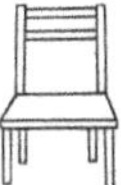

INTERROGATION IS A COMPLEX interpersonal process shaped by the personalities of the interrogator and the interrogatee. Basically, no two interrogations are the same. Any useful model of interrogation is built on a conceptual framework in which the key components are flexibility, individuality and constant adaptability. Keeping with the Law of Requisite Variety,[74] any successful model must generate a sound strategy for effective performance. Simply stated, this law suggests that in a competition between two processes within a closed system, the one with a greater variety of options will be successful. In the context of an interrogation, the individual with the larger number of available options, such as sound strategies, qualities, abilities, personality, will prevail. Thus, Jerry Richardson, in *The Magic of Rapport*, has rightly observed that it is of great importance that "the interrogator always has at least one more method of leveraging compliance than the interrogatee has for resisting."[75]

The Reid Technique of Interviewing and Interrogation—an interrogation process built on a conceptual framework of sound psychological principles—has been found to be most useful and successful. John Reid, along with Fred Inbau from Chicago, developed this model in 1974 when law enforcement agencies in the US and other countries faced criticism for the application of coercive methods of interrogation to obtain confessions from suspects. Massive human rights violations, especially of POWs and civil rights activists during the post World War II period, and new methods of interrogation used against Vietnamese soldiers and guerillas during the two-decade long Vietnam War (1955-1975), opened a Pandora's box of issues and controversies emphasizing the need for non-coercive tools in interrogations.

The Reid model involves three different components namely pre-interrogation fact- gathering and analysis, Behaviour Analysis Interview (BAI) and interrogation, which are separate and distinct procedures closely intertwined with any investigation. A thorough investigation and analysis of facts is essential to a successful interrogation. The Reid Technique emphasizes that the interrogator should conduct as much of the investigation as possible, collect a first-hand account of the offense or the incident and should not go by the reports of others. The fact analysis should cover the entire gamut of the crime or offense such as place and time of occurrence, legal nature of the offense, the details of victims, possible suspect or suspects with their biosocial profile and known weakness, motive(s) to commit the offense, crime-scene details and recoveries. The key element of fact analysis is an inductive approach in which each individual suspect of the offense is evaluated with respect to specific facts or observations relating to that particular crime or incident.

Let us discuss the concept of pre-interrogation fact analysis on the basis of a missing person case of a 20-year-old youth. The youth's father lodged a complaint at the nearest police station explaining the sequence of events leading to his disappearance along with details of half a dozen of his friends in the locality. The police interviewed three of his close friends who were subsequently let off, treating them as improbable suspects. They presented a convincing story that the youth, who was wanted in a drug-peddling case, had left the village fearing his detention. As there was no progress in tracing down the youth, the aggrieved father filed a habeas corpus petition, following which the police intensified the investigation. During the fact-gathering process, the new investigators further interviewed the father of the missing youth and collected all the minute details, including a leading clue that on the day of his disappearance, the youth had left the house in a two-wheeler driven by his juvenile friend. Later, the youth's dead body was found in a nearby marshy area. It soon came to light that the youth's close friends, who were initially interviewed by the police and subsequently let off, had committed the crime.

We can draw a few conclusions about fact analysis and the pre-interrogation interview here. First and foremost is the systematic effort of the investigator to collect as many details as possible about the crime or the incident, for which both open and secret enquiries can be undertaken. In offenses involving human beings, such as simple or grievous hurt, molestation or rape, the interrogators should first interview the victim or close relations, whose factual narration of the event or crime will allow them to narrow down the number of suspects. Secondly, the biosocial profile of all the suspects should be prepared by incorporating details such as gender, race, education, occupation, marital status, any weakness such as addictions to drugs, alcohol, gambling or over-indulgence in sex. The third element is the opportunity or access to commit the crime such as friendship, previous acquaintance, club member, gang member or similar. Fourthly, the investigators should look into the behaviour of the suspects before and after the offense. Some hardened criminals or habitual offenders act naturally and cover up the crime, as the friends of the missing youth had done in the case above. However, first-time offenders or juveniles unable to cover up feelings exhibit them in one way or another during interactions with the victim's relatives. In the same missing persons case, the police could make a breakthrough only after taking the juvenile into confidence through systematic interview. Finally, in identifying probable suspects or the innocent, investigators have to ascertain the motivation and propensity to commit the crime. This may be previous enmity, vendetta, frustration in love affairs, greediness to make quick money. In our case, one of the accused was convinced that the victim was responsible for the road accident and death of his brother—a member of the drug gang—and this led him to murder the youth. Through proper analysis of the facts and evidence gathered, the investigators can narrow down the number of suspects and be better placed to effectively confront the suspect(s) at the time of interrogation.

Though the pre-interrogation interview is designed to gather information about the offense, another major purpose of this exercise is to establish rapport with the suspect(s) and to assess their baseline behaviour. Thus, in the Reid model of interrogation, Behaviour Analysis Interview (BAI) or Behaviour Symptom Analysis (BSA) has crucial significance. The BAI involves evaluation of the verbal, paralinguistic and non-verbal responses to identify possibly guilty and deceptive suspects. It also helps the interrogators to determine whether they have to move from the interview stage to the interrogation stage. The Reid model also stipulates a number of basic principles that should be followed by the investigators while conducting the BAI. Firstly, they should know that there are no unique behaviours associated with truthfulness and deception. Secondly, they have to simultaneously evaluate all three channels of communication and responses (verbal, non-verbal and paralinguistic) before arriving at conclusions on the approach of the suspects(s). Finally, through BAI, the interrogators should try to establish the suspect's normal behaviour pattern.

The authors of the Reid model also prescribe certain important guidelines to evaluate a suspect's behaviour. Firstly, the interrogators should look for deviations from the suspect's normal behaviour. Once a normative behaviour is established, the subsequent changes that occur when the suspect is confronted with investigative questions will become important. Secondly, behavioural responses should be assessed on the basis of when they occur and how often they occur. The timing and consistency of responses are two reliable factors enabling interrogators to determine truthfulness or deception of the statements given by the suspect. The BAI is unique in several respects, the most important is its emphasis on using the baseline approach to behaviour evaluation. This baseline behaviour is determined through a fairly structured non-accusatory question-and-answer session with the suspect, before formally commencing the interrogation. Moreover, the Reid guidelines on BAI are also relevant to other interrogation models that determine the truthfulness and deception of suspects based on verbal and non-verbal responses during interrogation.

Nine steps of Reid Model interrogation: Central to the Reid model is a nine-step approach to interrogation. These steps provide interrogators clear sign posts and directions to organize the interrogation in a systematic and effective manner so as to elicit maximum information and evidence from the suspect. At the same time, the founders of the Reid model insist that not all these steps nor their sequence will be necessary or appropriate in every interrogation. Interrogators need to adopt different approaches depending upon the personality or behaviour of the suspect and plan the right technique after close observation and assessment of his or her behaviour and responses. For example, in the case of an emotional suspect, a sympathetic approach has been found to be more successful—expressing understanding and empathy in relation to his or her commission of the crime and present plight. On the other hand, if the offender is a hardened criminal or an extremist devoid of any repentance or guilt, a factual analysis approach is more effective confronting him or her with established facts and evidence of their involvement. Whether to interrogate a suspect is a consideration only when the investigator is reasonably certain of the suspect's involvement in the crime under investigation. The decision is made after interviewing all possible suspects and evaluating their inputs in terms of access, motive, alibi, and concluding that a particular suspect has committed the offense.

Step 1: Positive Confrontation. The interrogator confronts the suspect with a brief, exact and unequivocal statement of crime or offence and closely observes verbal and non-verbal responses to determine much of how the interrogation proceeds. At the same time, he offers a compelling reason for the suspect to tell the truth. The deceptive suspect will usually lower his eyes, change posture and move in the chair and offer a vague denial. The innocent or truthful suspect demonstrates body language suggesting innocence and replies in a very direct and spontaneous fashion. In both cases, the interrogator repeats the initial statement of involvement.

Step 2: Theme Development. The interrogator presents some specific suppositions or explanations (theme) about the reason for the crime, in which the suspect should be offered a possible moral excuse for having committed the offense. For example, in the missing youth case that we discussed earlier, the interrogators tactfully used the theme that it is quite natural that in operations like drug peddling that the gang leaders would never pardon those partners betraying the gang. However, while presenting the theme, the interrogator should not plant new ideas in the deceptive suspect's mind, but rather let the suspect feel more comfortable talking about his crime by allowing him to reduce the perceived consequences associated with it. It is equally important that the interrogator presents the theme in a natural, empathetic and understanding manner, discouraging the suspect from lengthy arguments or discussions that will deter him from telling the truth.

Step 3: Handling Denials. Almost all suspects, innocent or guilty, will attempt to deny their involvement in the offense or incident. Depending on the nature and persistence of the denials, the interrogator may become convinced of the suspect's actual innocence or secondary role. In general, an innocent person will not allow the denials to be cut off. Innocent denials will strengthen over time and the suspect will begin to assert control over the interrogation. He remains steadfast in the assertion of his innocence. The sincerity with which he presents his case is a clear indication of his truthfulness. Once the interrogator is convinced of the suspect's innocence, he should begin to modify the intensity of his position and try to elicit other information that would be helpful to reach the real offender(s), such as the suspect's own suspicions about other persons who were involved in the crime. A guilty individual will eventually submit to the investigator's return to a theme. In such cases, the interrogator should cut off the denials, discourage them, evaluate the suspect's responses for indications of truthfulness and attempt to return to the selected themes.

Step 4: Overcoming Objections. When a guilty suspect feels that his attempts to deny his involvement in the crime are unsuccessful, he will try to assert some control over the interrogators by raising objections that he thinks will support his innocence. Usually, there are three types of objections: emotional, factual and moral. Instead of rejecting these objections or entering into an argument with the suspect, the interrogator should accept them as if true but use them to his advantage. If the interrogator is successful in overcoming a suspect's objections, the suspect will psychologically withdraw and begin to focus his thoughts on the impending punishment.

Step 5: Procurement and Retention of Suspect's Attention. If the interrogator shows no signs of being convinced by the suspect's objections, the only strategy left for a guilty suspect who does not want to tell the truth is to psychologically withdraw from the interrogation. He may become quiet, withdrawn and pensive. In order to procure and retain the withdrawn suspect's attention, the interrogator should move his chair closer to the suspect, establish and maintain eye contact, use visual aids and use hypothetical questions, since we are all conditioned to respond to questions.

Step 6: Handling the Suspect's Pensive Mood. The suspect who realizes the futility of his efforts to conceal his offense through denials or objections, becomes reticent and quiet, often adopting a defiant posture, but at the same time becoming more willing to listen. Many suspects feeling defeated or pensive may begin to cry, which is an indication of their feelings of remorse. In general, the suspect will appear passive, downcast and depressed. The interrogator should now start to distil the possible reasons for the crime presented in the theme and concentrate on the core of the selected theme. This approach is supplemented by urging and advising the suspect to tell the truth, moving closer to the suspect and continuing to display understanding and sympathy.

Step 7: Presenting an Alternative Question. When the suspect is totally pensive or silent, the interrogator's task is to bring him out of that mood and prompt him to tell the truth. We should not expect a suspect to abruptly break down and parrot the complete truth about the offense; instead, the interrogator uses the right tactics to encourage the suspect to initially make an admission of crime and then prompt him to unravel the whole truth or episode. A common tactic is to pose an alternative question, which essentially constitutes two incriminatory choices connected with the crime. The alternative question should be framed as a logical extension from the main theme. For example, in the missing youth case, as we discussed earlier, the alternative question can be: "Is this the first time that you targeted him, or have you made previous attempts?" The suspect, in a pensive mood, finds in it as an escape route and makes a choice of saying "the first time," which reflects his inclination to admit the crime. In some instances, the interrogator makes a supporting statement—a statement which will help the suspect to choose the more sympathetic side of the alternative. In the above case, one of the interrogators posed the supporting question, "I think this is the first time, isn't it?" The suspect's mere nod may indicate his first admission of guilt. According to some critics of the Reid model, the alternate question tactic forces the suspect to incriminate himself, but proponents of Reid point out that the suspect always has a third choice, which is to say that neither alternative is true.

Step 8: Oral Detailing of the Offense by the Suspect. Once the suspect admits to an alternative question, the interrogator's immediate task is to obtain confirmation of the suspect's admission of guilt. This involves a brief oral review of the basic sequence of events involved in the crime with sufficient detail to corroborate the suspect's guilt. At this stage, the interrogator's questions should be brief, concise and clear. Once the suspect narrates the entire episode, the interrogator picks up on contradictions and asks for clarifications—questions that will reinforce evidence.

Step 9: Converting an Oral Narration into a Confession. Depending upon the nature of crime or the agencies involved in the interrogation process, different formats are adopted for recording confessions. In criminal investigations, the suspect writes the confession statement, which is read back to him and signed (sometimes in the presence of a witness). In some other instances, a statement written by the interrogator is subsequently read and signed by the suspect. Audio-recorded or video-recorded statements are also in practice. Normally, intelligence agencies do not record interrogation statements in the presence of the accused. Instead, they prepare a consolidated interrogation statement after the interrogation is over.

The Kinesic Model was introduced by Frederick Link and Foster Glenn of the US in the late 1970s. This model also uses a pre-interrogation approach along the lines of the BAI adopted in the Reid technique. This process is called Practical Kinesic Analysis Phase (PKAP), which involves an analysis of the suspect's behaviour to detect deception, discomfort and unusual sensitivity. Like the BAI, the PKAP examines behaviour related to verbal quality, verbal content and non-verbal responses on the basis of two basic principles—no single behaviour, by itself, proves anything and there is no universally accepted behaviour in any form that proves a person is being truthful or deceptive.

Kinesic interrogation, just like the Reid method, is a continuation of the initial interview. Like the other techniques, this model also recognizes that the interrogator cannot depend on a singular, standardized approach to interrogation that can be applied to all types of suspects. A successful, practical Kinesic interrogation requires appropriate assessment of the suspect's dominant personality, such as introvert or extrovert or other sub-categories. Depending upon the personality of the suspect, the interrogators plan the right tactic or strategy. First, the interrogator makes the interrogation attack, confronting the suspect with the accusation and perhaps the evidence. In Kinesic interrogation, rapport building is only necessary if the suspect has an introverted personality, while the extrovert can be confronted in a more formal, business-like manner. Either way, the suspect is expected to react with one of several defence mechanisms (DMs). The interrogator must deactivate or neutralize these DMs by properly identifying the suspect's subconscious miscues that appear in the form of verbal and non-verbal responses. By properly deciphering these miscues and assessing the suspect's state of mind, the interrogator can confront him with further questions, leading to his confession or admission of guilt. Walters,[76] who set various rules and prescriptions for pushing the suspect to confession, highlighted that a successful Kinesic interrogation requires the interrogator to correctly identify and respond to the subject's five basic stress-response states—anger, depression, denial, bargaining and acceptance.

Proper detection of deception or truthfulness in the suspect's statements is based on eight basic principles, commonly described as the 8Cs of Kinesic analysis. These include:

1. Consistency: Behaviours or responses that are relatively consistent, in response to certain specific questions relating to the offense, are construed as truthful.

2. Constant: The normal or baseline behaviour of the suspect is assessed by asking non-threatening questions and observing the suspect's unstressed behaviour.

3. Change: Variations or change from baseline behaviour during investigative questions are important to assess truthful and deceptive behaviour of the suspect.

4. Cluster: These observed changes in the subject's baseline behaviours are diagnosed in clusters, not individually.

5. Contradictions: These include noticeable conflicts between verbal and non-verbal responses, retraction of a statement, stammering or stuttering.

6. Contamination: An interrogator's behaviour that may influence the accused's behaviour, which may then not be honest or truthful.

7. Preconception: An interrogator's preconceived notions or biased approach may impact accurate analysis of the suspect's responses.

8. Cross-check: Need to interpret a suspect's behaviour and disclosures based on change or contradictions noticed during the interrogation.

In his empirical studies on behaviours exhibited by suspects during deception, Aldert Vrij[92] has identified three general trends that will be useful for interrogators. For verbal characteristics, Vrij found that liars tend to have a higher-pitched voice than truth-tellers, and they seem to pause for longer when they speak than truth-tellers do. For non-verbal indicators, liars tend to move their arms, hands, fingers, feet and legs less than truth-tellers do. Vrij has identified seven characteristics of a good liar—being well prepared; being original; thinking quickly; being eloquent; having a good memory; not experiencing feelings of fear, guilt of duping or delight while lying; and being a good actor. In order to overcome a good liar's deceit and to detect deceptions, Vrij emphasized that interrogators should be suspicious, probe-oriented, discreet, informative and possess skills for close observation, cross-questioning and introspection. According to him, "the best hopes for lie detection in Kinesic are found in observing both emotional expressions and those behaviours influenced by content complexity (latency period, speech errors, speech hesitations, hand, arm, foot and leg movements)."

Preparation and Planning, Engage and Explain, Account, Closure and Evaluate (PEACE) Method: While the Reid model of interrogation was used ideally by investigation and law enforcement agencies in the US, many countries were sceptical of it for different reasons. According to Icelandic-British psychoanalyst and criminologist Gisli Gudjonsson, Britain implicitly rejected the model due to judicial decisions in cases involving oppressive interrogation methods, research findings of false confessions, psychological vulnerability and police and judicial reforms. Moreover, the use of interrogation tactics such as sensory deprivation, rigorous exercise, withholding of food and water and other oppressive methods during the anti-terror operations in Northern Ireland had evoked widespread public criticism and protests in many parts of Britain. These developments led to the introduction of the Police and Criminal Evidence Act (PACE) of 1984 and the Codes of Practice for Police Officers. These legislations discouraged coercive methods of interrogation and banned the use of deception, trickery and psychological exploitation in interrogation. New guidelines were formulated for interviewing witnesses and interrogating suspects.

The outcome of these reforms in the criminal justice system was the PEACE model of interrogation. It is a less confrontational method commonly used by law enforcement agencies. The PEACE approach was based on providing officers an ethical foundation for police questioning. It focuses on information gathering and relies on non-coercive interviewing and accurate recording of the interview to achieve its goals. As part of collecting facts, even the investigators or interrogators undertake crime scene visits to make enquiries and gather specific details, including the profile of suspects. The steps of this method are:

1. **Preparation and Planning:** During this phase, interrogators formulate the aims and objectives of the interrogation and their order. Other details of the plan may include the time a suspect has been in custody, the topics to be covered and specific points necessary to prove the offense. Preparing a biosocial profile of the accused that indicates his or her

habits and weakness, will help interrogators adopt the right strategies during interrogation.

2. **Engage and Explain:** Interrogators engage the suspect by explaining the reasons for the interrogation and its objectives. They patiently listen to the story and establish rapport with the suspect, who should be encouraged to divulge the truth on the plea that he or she will not get a chance to clear their position.

3. **Account:** Interrogators use two methods for eliciting an account of the offense or incident from the suspect. With cooperative suspects, they use a technique called cognitive interview to collect a true account of the facts connected with the crime through a process of retrieval of their memory. When the cognitive interview does not work, in the case of uncooperative suspects, they use conversation management. Interrogators use brief questions so that the suspect can clarify and expand their account. They should demonstrate patience and listen to the suspect's complete story, even if there are inconsistencies or contradictions.

4. **Closure:** The interrogator summarizes the main points from the interview and provides the suspect with the opportunity to correct or add information. Just like a bank cashier closing a day's account after painstakingly tallying the credits and disbursal, the interrogators summarize the main points and give the suspect an opportunity to correct and add information. Caution should be taken not to end this phase abruptly.

5. **Evaluate:** Interrogators assess how the account given by the suspect fits into the investigation as a whole, how far the missing links can be collected and strengthened, whether

any further action is needed and how effective and useful the interrogation was.

Besides these main models (Reid, Kinesic and PEACE), criminologists and psychoanalysts have developed other methods of interrogation. One such leading model is the **Psychoanalytic Model** developed by Swedish psychoanalyst Gunnar Berggren[77] on the basis of psychoanalytical studies by other eminent psychoanalysts like Gudjonsson and Theodor Reik.[78] Based on Freudian concepts of the id and ego, they found that the unconscious compulsion to confess plays a seminal role in crime. The confession, according to them, is "an attempt at reconciliation that the superego undertakes in order to settle the quarrel between the ego and the id." In a nutshell, the model postulates that people's knowledge of their transgression produces a sense of guilt that is experienced as oppressive and distressing. The role of the interrogator is to exploit this psychological element and prompt the suspect to confess and get rid of the feeling of guilt.

Another popular method is **Interaction Process Model**, in which the suspect's initial responses and the final outcome of the interrogation are determined by the interaction of three factors: a) the background characteristics of the suspect and the offense, b) the extent of evidence against the suspect and his access to legal advice and c) the interrogation techniques used by the interrogators. Empirical studies by criminologists and researchers like Moston, Stephenson and Williamson[79] proved that most admissions were freely volunteered at the outset of interviews, and those suspects who denied an accusation at the outset typically maintained this denial throughout, even in the face of seemingly incontrovertible proof of guilt.

Next is the **Cognitive-Behavioural Model**: Psychoanalyst and criminologist Gudjonsson espoused this model based on his finding that confessions are the result of "the existence of a particular relationship between the suspect, the environment and significant others within that environment."[80] The model suggests that antecedents (events occurring prior to interrogation) and consequences (effects of a confession) influence the confessional behaviour of a suspect. These antecedents and consequences are construed in terms of social, emotional, cognitive, situational and physiological events. Social influence relates to the isolation of the suspect from his or her family and friends. The interrogation manuals prescribe that the suspect's isolation from any external influence may reduce his or her willingness to confess. In the case of emotional influence, arrest and detention in a cell lead to a lot of stress and strain, created mainly by the uncertainty of the situation and the fear of what will happen at the detention place. Cognitive factors comprise the suspect's thoughts, interpretations, assumptions and perceived strategies of responding to the interrogative situation. According to Gudjonsson, a suspect's behaviour during the interrogation is likely to be more influenced by his or her perceptions, interpretations and assumptions about what is happening than by the actual behaviour of the interrogators. Situational influences can be indefinite, ranging from the circumstances of arrest, place and condition of confinement, treatment by personnel at various places. The physiological antecedent to a confession is heightened arousal, which includes increased heart rate and blood pressure, irregularity of respiration and increased perspiration.

Another model is the **Decision-Making Model** espoused by Hilgendorf and Irving[81] and based on the basic principle that a suspect's decision or confession is made not in a vacuum, but through a number of prevailing conditions and circumstances that influence his or her decision-making process. Prominent factors include: the offense under investigation, characteristics of the interrogators, interrogation settings, profile and personality traits of the suspect such as experiences, competencies, knowledge, skills, beliefs, expectations and script. Consequently, the suspect's decisions are determined by his perceptions of the available courses of action—perceptions concerning the probabilities or consequences attached to action and the utility values or gains attached to these courses of action.

Finally, there is the **Dialogue Model**, an alternative and less traditional model espoused by Douglas Walton[82] who conceives of interrogation as a dialogue between the suspect and interrogator. In many respects, it is a modified conversation. Unlike a traditional critical conversation broken into different phases where both the parties decide to switch from one stage to the next, in traditional interrogation, the interrogator unilaterally decides and proceeds into the different stages of interrogation, which are formative, preparatory, argumentation and closing. Inevitably, it is an asymmetrical dialogue, in which the interrogator dominates the conversation and the suspect tends to be very passive. Accordingly, Walton recommends that the interrogator needs to appear friendly and cooperative, even sympathetic to the suspect—be patient, methodical, repeat unanswered questions and be prepared to continue the interrogation for an indefinite period of time. He also suggests a number of techniques such as "the easiest way out" (creating an impression that suspect's problems will be over once he confesses or furnishes the required inputs) or "the only way out (a technique in which the interrogator makes the conditions unbearable for the suspect). Walton also points out that other suitable techniques such as catching the suspect off guard, misrepresenting the law, diluting the seriousness of the offense or using coercive methods can be used to elicit information from the suspect.

On close analysis, the models of interrogations above are based on the complex interrelations between mind and body that manifest through distinct physical and metabolic changes under special circumstances or situations. The underlying principle is that under stress or strain created through systematic questioning, the suspect will exhibit distinct physical, psychological or verbal behaviours, based on which interrogators can arrive at conclusions on their involvement or otherwise in a specific crime or offence. In William Sargant's words, "The stress that the interrogators put on the subject causes distinct and predictable physiological effects that result in the subject losing his or her previous sets of beliefs."[83] This change in belief ultimately leads to a confession. Considering the complexities of the human mind, as unravelled by psychologists and psychoanalysts, one pertinent question is about the reliability or authenticity of such changes or the confessions by suspects under stress.

Against the backdrop of such questions, the Reid and Kinesic models of interrogation have provoked major criticism. According to legal experts and researchers like Steven A Drizin and Richard A Leo, the Reid method is based on certain assumptions about human behaviour that are not supported by empirical evidence. They argue that false confessions by the accused had underscored the major pitfalls of these commonly accepted interrogation models. The infamous Central Park Five jogger case of 1989, which rocked New York City, questioned the infallibility of interrogation models as the five juveniles who made voluntary confessions during interrogation and were found guilty and jailed for the crime were subsequently proven innocent.

Similarly, the sensational murder case of Stephanie Crowe of Escondido, California, in 1998 and the false confessions of three juveniles during interrogation evoked widespread public debate and awareness on problematic police interrogation techniques leading to false confessions and miscarriage of justice. In this case, 14-year-old Michael Crowe, the brother of the victim (Stephanie), was initially suspected of the murder. He succumbed to the pressure and falsely confessed after nine hours of intense interrogation, including the infallible Computer Voice Stress Analyzer test. Joshua Treadway, Michael's friend and suspected co-perpetrator in the crime was interrogated for about 22 hours. He, too, confessed along the lines of Michael's confession. Another juvenile friend of Michael, Aaron Houser, also similarly confessed. Fortunately for the trio, their innocence was established when Stephanie's blood was discovered on the sweatshirt of a homeless drifter, Richard Tuite, who was subsequently tried and convicted. Ironically, the police had taken Tuite in custody immediately after the crime occurred, questioned him, but let him off on the basis of his statement. However, the police retained his sweatshirt and subsequent DNA testing helped the police to establish his involvement in the crime. The inadequacy of legal mechanisms to avert such tragedies came under sharp criticism and these developments paved the way for extensive research on various interrogation techniques.

One of the main themes of this research was the reliability of interrogators to detect a suspect's deception. The researchers found that behaviour or response styles of suspects during interrogation cannot be fully relied upon to identify the truth from deception. It was also established that interrogators who depend on non-verbal or linguistic clues as indicators are prone to error.

They broadly classified such errors as misclassification errors, coercion errors and contamination errors. Misclassification begins when investigators consciously or unconsciously target an innocent person as suspect. They act like human lie detectors and pick up suspects based on certain observations or assumptions, which may or may not be true. Such things happen in sensational cases with much public rhetoric or pressure to detain the accused. Once the suspect is identified, investigators, sometimes assisted by prosecutors, select and filter the evidence that will build a case for conviction while ignoring or suppressing evidence that points away from guilt. Thus, in many cases, interrogators easily overlook or dismiss any statement or disclosure by the suspect that is inconsistent with the chosen theory, attributing it as irrelevant, unreliable or incredible. In interrogation parlance, this approach is termed tunnel vision, which on many occasions leads to the arrest and incarceration of innocent people.

Coercion errors usually occur in the case of high-profile suspects in sensational cases. They cannot withstand the psychological coercion by interrogators and easily accept their demands or the alleged findings. The sole motive for their admission or confession would be to escape the heat or pressure of interrogation. Many times, interrogators evoke the ordeal of their close relatives or associates in order to psychologically exploit the accused and get their admission of guilt. The third factor is the vulnerability of the accused. Usually, first-time offenders or juveniles placed under the stress and strain created by interrogators, easily succumb to the pressure and admit guilt. Perhaps the best example is the

Stephanie Crowe case mentioned previously, in which all three juveniles accused, despite their non-involvement in the crime, confessed to the tune of their investigators. Researchers have established that a number of factors such as age, gender, ethnic differences, mental state and psychological factors and previous convictions influence whether a suspect will confess or disclose incriminating information.

Finally, the contamination error is very common, especially in interrogation models like Reid. When the interrogators present non-public information related to the offense to a suspect or accused, many suspects endorse such information and make a confession along those lines. A classic case for this was EJ Lowery v. the County of Riley.[84] In many cases, interrogators exploit the mental condition of the accused through coercive tactics so that he or she will easily acknowledge the interrogator's version of events.

9

Types of Questions and the Art of Questioning

THOMAS SAMUEL KUHN, THE famous American historian and philosopher of the twentieth century said, "the answers you get depend on the questions you ask." In the context of interrogation, Kuhn's words are exceedingly relevant, as the success of any interrogation depends considerably on the types of questions and the order in which the questions are asked. Dillon[85] has classified the types of questions used during interrogation. The type of questions and the approach of questioning vary from suspect to suspect, and vary across the pre-interrogation interview and the interrogation phase. However, following are some of the common types of questions used for interrogation.

Open-ended questions: Interrogators usually start with open-ended questions that allow the suspect to freely provide information. These questions elicit longer narratives that help develop an open conversation, which enables the interrogator to find out more details connected with the incident. A good interrogator later switches over to the funnel method and seeks more specifics, focusing on who, what, when, where, why, and how—"the famous six servants of Rudyard Kipling."[86] While trying to extract specifics, the investigator poses pointed questions such as "Who told you that?" and "What did she say to you?" and "Where were you during this conversation?" and "How did that make you feel?" and "What happened next?" Based on experience, properly framed open-ended questions are always better and preferable to dig out more details or even the actual truth from a suspect during interrogation.

Funnel Questions: As mentioned above, funnel questions usually start with a general or an open-ended question and subsequently drill down to a more specific point in each. Usually, this will involve asking for more and more details at each level. Assume an investigator trying to identify Diana, who supplied heroin at a party. Let us examine how the interrogator undertakes this task using funnel questions while interrogating a suspect who attended the party.

Question: Tell me how you celebrated the New Year?

Answer: We had a dinner party at Tom's house.

Question: How many people were there at the dinner party?

Answer: About 15.

Question: Were they all men or women?

Answer: Mostly men.

Question: How many women?

Answer: 4 or 5.

Question: Did any of them wear anything distinctive?

Answer: Yes, 2 of them had red jackets.

Question: Can you recollect if there was anything special on those jackets?

Answer: Yes, the slim lady's jacket had a wolf symbol.

Question: Who was that slim lady?

Answer: She was Diana from Male.

Based on these disclosures, the investigators can very well fix the identity of Diana, who is suspected to be the kingpin of a drug syndicate that supplied drugs at the New Year party.

Closed questions: These questions usually generate a single word or a very short, factual answer. For example, "Are you thirsty?" gets the answer either yes or no. "Where do you live?" and the answer is generally the name of your town or your address. At the same time, a misplaced closed question can spoil the tempo of the interrogation and lead to awkward silence from the suspect. For example, "Did you try to molest the girl at the club party?"

Yes or No questions: These are modified closed questions for which the answer is either positive or negative. For example, "Did you force her to enter your car?" The answer may be yes or no.

Multiple-choice questions: These are questions with more than one option as the answer. For example, "What dress was she wearing—a sari, a gown or jeans with a top?"

Tag questions: Tag questions can be used when the suspect is stating a claim but lacks full confidence in the truth of that statement. For instance, the statement is "The city is a den of drug traffickers." The tag question could be, "The city is a den of drug traffickers, isn't it?"

Indicator questions: These involve some hint related to the event or offense. Such questions are based on a concrete piece of evidence or witness statement. For example, "If your friend says that he saw you in the park, would you have any explanation?"

Precise questions: A precise question is one that calls for a specific or an exact answer. It limits the requested answer to a definite item of information. It is almost similar to a yes or no question.

Discerning questions: Discerning questions are questions designed to produce information directly related to the matter being discussed. They are questions that discriminate between what is relevant and what is irrelevant.

Certain types of questions should be avoided during interrogation. They include:

Leading questions: As far as possible, interrogators should avoid leading questions as well as opinion questions. Both types are weak and ineffective techniques because they introduce the interrogator's ideas or assumptions and provide the suspect with a preconceived approach that he can follow. In fact, through this process, interrogators put words into the suspect's mouth who in turn vomits the same to the full satisfaction of the interrogators. Such practices destroy the basic ethics and sanctity of interrogation. Examples include, "Did you use a red car to hit the person?" and "Did you carry a revolver while stepping out of his car?" Instead of such leading questions, interrogators can reframe their inquiry as, "How was the victim hit near the park?" and "Did you carry anything while getting out of the car?"

Leading compound questions: This question may contain preferred answers, but will be compound in nature. For instance, "Did you notice any stranger with her or was she was alone there?"

Loaded questions: A loaded question contains presuppositions such that when the suspect gives a direct answer to the question, he concedes certain assumptions that were made and that are damaging to his interests. Loaded questions are different from leading questions. While leading questions prompt the suspect to provide a specific answer, loaded questions are considered trick questions because they assume something about the suspect within the question itself. For example, David is interrogated on a charge of calling Maria a racial slur. During the interrogation, interrogators may desist from asking, "What slur did you call Maria?" If such a question is asked, the inference is that he (David) actually used a slur. Instead, the question should be framed as, "Share what you discussed with Maria during your personal meeting with her?"

But as Dillon points out, in some cases, complex and loaded questions can be used, provided they occur in the right order in a sequence of dialogue, for example, suppose that in an interrogation, the suspect just admitted that he had tortured his spouse. Asking the complex and loaded question, "Have you stopped torturing your spouse?" could be quite appropriate here. Fallacious questioning tends to occur when the interrogators or the suspect is unaware of the complex or loaded nature of a question, and misleading conclusions are drawn from the asking and answering of such a question.[87] The loaded question is also a key component of the Reid technique's step 7 (presenting an alternative theme or question), thus showing the utility of such questions in the interrogation setting.

Loophole questions: These are questions posed by some interrogators at the end of the narration of a theme or a specific disclosure by the suspect. Most commonly, they ask, "Is there anything you want to add?" Sometimes, such questions evoke doubts in the suspect's mind that his or her disclosures (even truthful) did not convince or satisfy the interrogators. Thus, smart suspects weave fabricated stories or additional disclosures to impress the interrogators. In one specific example of a sensational investigation, when interrogators consistently posed such questions to the suspect (a senior scientist), he wove a convincing story based on his old acquaintances and contacts who worked in sensitive establishments or held senior positions in different organizations. His narrative, which had all the ingredients of an espionage story, was taken as a true confession that changed the course of future investigations.

Royal and Schutt[88] have highlighted certain fundamental characteristics of good question construction for an interrogation. Their suggestions include: a) questions should be short and confined to one topic; b) they should be clear and easily understood; c) to avoid using frightening words such as murderer, forger, drug addict, embezzler, confession, drunkard, etc., and instead to use mild and polished words and phrases; and d) use precise and clear questions.

In *The Practice of Questioning*, Dillon suggests that questions should be prepared beforehand and written down on paper. However, a majority of other authors do not endorse his suggestion on the grounds that pre-prepared questions inhibit the flexibility and natural tempo of questioning. Usually, such advance questionnaires for interrogation are used only in a few instances, such as the questioning of very important persons (VIPs) in cases of corruption, or for those accused or remanded for a very brief period. Such questioning fails to make much headway in the investigation of such cases as the suspects, backed by legal experts, keep silent or give evasive replies.

But Dillon's classification of different types of questions and their appropriate order during the different stages of interrogation has been found to be useful in all types of interrogation. According to him, interrogators should start with opening questions that do not contain anything about the crime or the purpose of interrogation. Preferably, they may be yes or no facilitator-type questions, to which the suspect can easily respond. One basic aim of such questions is to establish rapport with the suspect. The next phase is open-ended free narrative questions, in which the interrogator simply names a theme connected with the offense and asks the suspect to narrate what he knows about it. An example is the question, "I understand you were present when the dinner was going on, so would you please describe what happened." The interrogator should then listen to the reply without interrupting. A direct question follows up a narrative question by asking about a specific item. This is almost like the funnel method in which the interrogator digs out specific answers. According to Dillon, experience has proved that it is best to avoid value-laden terms when asking direct questions. He highlights two examples. "An actual rapist will admit having sex with a woman but will deny raping her." Or, "Tough guys fight somebody, not assault and battery them." So, he emphasizes that the interrogator should stick to language that directly describes the actions at issue instead of using value-laden language that imputes guilt. Thus, Walton[89] holds that since language in a criminal investigation tends to be laden with ethical values, interrogators should try to rephrase questions in a more direct way that removes these emotive connotations of the words. An agile interrogator picks up on contradictions during the narrative stage and uses **cross questions** to probe into ambiguous, vague, evasive or apparently contradictory answers. **Review questions** are appropriate at the closing stage. These are just like tag questions, meant to confirm previous answers, as in the question, "Is that correct?" Authors like Dillion highlight that small talk with the suspect at the closing stage could facilitate an alert interrogator to get useful clues that might be dropped by the suspect in the form of unguarded statements made in casual remarks. Interrogators who establish better rapport with juveniles or first-time offenders use such tactics to get additional inputs or clues helpful for the investigation.

The type of questions and the style of questioning differ across the pre-interrogation interview and during interrogation.

All models of interrogation emphasize the need for an initial interview, which has the dual purpose of gathering information and building rapport with the suspect. For example, Behavioural Analysis Interview (BAI) is intended to assess the baseline behavioural approach of a suspect and is a significant phase of the Reid technique of interrogation. In fact, this stage is so crucial in the Reid model that it determines whether or not to move into the interrogation. Thus, Aubry[90] has rightly commented, "nearly all interrogations which eventually fail for whatever given reason, have actually failed due to lapses during the first few moments of the interview." Royal and Schutt[91] write that, "resistance to the disclosure of information is considerably increased if the interrogator is a total stranger, or if something is not done to establish a friendly and trusting attitude on the part of the suspect." Through a pre-interrogation interview, the interrogator establishes initial rapport with the suspect.

An interview is defined as the questioning of a respondent who is "ready, willing and able to tell what he knows." He or she may be a suspect or witness. Basically, an investigative interview is neither fully informal or formal, but lies somewhere in the middle. The crucial issue here is that the interviewers ask the right kind of questions. The questions should be non-accusatory, freely flowing and relatively unstructured, but should be designed to gather information. Preferably singular, non-compound questions should be asked. As far as possible, interrogators should avoid compound questions, which can be confusing. A compound question essentially consists of many questions disguised and combined into one question. For example, "Who told you that and what did she say?" is an example of a compound question because it simultaneously seeks information about "who" made the statement and "what" was said.

Though the interview and the interrogation are information-seeking processes, they differ both in the attitude of the respondent and the approach of the questioners. In an investigative interview, the suspect or witness may be more willing and cooperative whereas in an interrogation, the suspect or accused may be hostile, reluctant and unwilling to divulge information. As rightly pointed out by Walton, "Interrogation in and of itself creates a power disparity between the person asking the question (interrogator) and the person being questioned (suspect or accused). The interrogator has the right to control the subject matter, tempo and progress of the questioning, to interrupt responses to questions and to judge whether the responses are satisfactory. The person questioned, on the other hand, has no right to question the interrogator, or even to question the propriety of the questions the interrogator has posed." These factors considerably influence the style of questioning during interview and interrogation.

In an investigative interview, an effective investigator will put the interviewee at ease in order to elicit as much information as possible. Vrij[92] suggests that during the interview, the investigator must be open-minded and flexible, should establish rapport and should provide little to no information about the case to avoid making it easier for the suspect to lie or come up with explanations. The Reid technique also emphasizes interview for establishing rapport and trust with the suspect, as well as to learn information about the suspect that will help to formulate the right techniques during interrogation. For that purpose, the investigator should frame proper interview questions, allow the interviewee plenty of time to respond, exhibit patience and avoid frequent interruption. Rather than a questioner, he should be a listener. Many experienced investigators hold that the best follow-up question in an interview is no question at all. They should allow the suspect to fill the void of silence by speaking more and providing more information. More often than not, an investigator who utilizes the power of silence for a moment prior to asking the next question will reap the benefits. Above all, the investigator must maintain professionalism so that the interviewee responds seriously and honestly.

A properly conducted pre-interrogation interview allows the investigators to make an initial assessment of the suspect—such as his or her communications skills, general nervous tension, normal level of eye contact and a behavioural baseline. At the same time, it also helps the suspect evaluate the interrogators, especially their professionalism, commitment, knowledge and unbiased approach. Based on these factors, experienced interrogators work out their technique and the question-and-answer pattern during interrogation, whereas the suspect decides their approach towards the interrogators. Once the interrogator assesses the personality, temperament and behavioural makeup of the suspect, he must quickly determine the approach that would be most useful for this type of suspect. The interrogator must appear sympathetic, sincere, impartial, empathetic and firm, all at the same time. Aubry emphasizes the importance of even the investigator's entrance into the interrogation room. He holds, "he must (enter) with an intangible air which adds up to confidence, confidence in himself, and confidence in his ability to carry out a successful interrogation; he must exude this air of confidence."[93] He should also demonstrate an air of resolution and firmness, which however, should not leave an impression in suspect's mind that the interrogator is out to get him at all costs.

For the success of the interrogation, interrogators should maintain proper body language and verbal responses. Improper body movements or facial expressions or out-of-context verbal responses will send wrong signals to the suspect who, on many occasions, takes inexperienced interrogators for a ride, virtually defeating the purpose of the interrogation. Interrogators should keep their facial expression neutral and adopt a gentleman-like posture during the interrogation and should not get carried away by the interrogatee's emotional outbursts. Equally important is the interrogator's ability to properly decipher the suspect's verbal and non-verbal responses and to reach accurate conclusions or assessments, especially regarding the suspect's truthfulness or deception. Once the suspect's normative behaviour has been established during the pre-interrogation interview, subsequent changes that occur when the suspect is interrogated about the offense will become significant. Such deviations or changes need to be evaluated on the basis of timing and consistency. To be reliable indicators of truth or deception, behavioural changes should occur immediately in response to questions or simultaneously with the suspect's answers. Furthermore, similar behavioural responses should occur on a consistent basis, or in other words, whenever the same subject matter is discussed.

10

Actual Phase of Interrogation

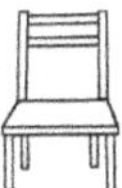

ONCE THE INTERROGATION ROOM is properly arranged, the formal interrogation begins. Depending on the nature of the offense or the suspect, the complexion of the team is decided. An ideal interrogation team should consist of at least three members who have details about the offense and the background of the interrogatee. Normally in criminal or law enforcement interrogations, the officer in charge of the investigation may head the team as he or she is well-versed with the facts of the case and areas of core evidence that should be collected during the interrogation. In the case of counterintelligence suspects or terrorists or extremists, joint interrogation teams comprising members of different agencies would undertake interrogation. In such cases, prior interaction among team members is salutary for ensuring better synergy and coordination during interrogation, as the perspective and priorities of agencies differ depending upon their charter or areas of operations.

To begin with, allow the suspect or accused to speak, which will enable the interrogators to ascertain how truthful he or she is. The team can also let the accused tell a few lies based on which the interrogators can build up suitable themes to confront the interrogatee. Interrogators should develop skills to closely focus and follow what the suspect or accused communicates through eye contact, verbal and non-verbal responses. Experienced interrogators can deduce valuable clues or inferences out of such responses and signs. In many instances, when interrogators take notes during interrogation, they fail to maintain eye contact with the interrogatee and to decipher the non-verbal and verbal responses. Moreover, the accused becomes more defensive in the presence of interrogators taking down notes.

Thus, the best approach is to memorize important disclosures of the accused. Interrogators do this through a process of mental filtering—eliminating unwanted or irrelevant disclosures from memory and focusing on the core elements of the statement. After all, a sharp memory is an asset for a good interrogator. Alternatively, clandestine videography or audio recording can be resorted to in the case of sensitive interrogations involving terrorists or espionage agents. Recorded statements are highly useful for proper analysis (especially of verbal-non-verbal responses) to appropriately confront the interrogatee and for follow-up enquiries.

An interrogator's discretion also matters a lot. Just like experienced interrogators do, trained agents or habitual offenders quickly develop their impressions of the interrogators and accordingly adapt their tactics to not divulge the truth. For example, frequent breaks in eye contact with the accused give him the impression that the interrogators are not focused or serious in their approach. On the other hand, when interrogators adopt consistent posture with constant eye contact, the accused forms an impression that the interrogators are fully and seriously involved in the process. Interrogators should not give any hint, formally or informally, to the interrogatee about the duration of the interrogation. At the same time, they should emphasize for the suspect that the interrogation will go on till the whole truth is out.

The interrogator's tone of voice is equally important in maintaining proper tempo. A natural and pleasing voice with proper modulation, demonstrating the right amount of concern and involvement, helps to establish better rapport with the suspect. On the other hand, sudden bullying or barking tones create a strong mental block in the suspect's mind.

Patience and a keen listening capacity help interrogators get the maximum out of suspects. Too much talk or lengthy discussions or debates seldom help interrogators get the truth out of the suspect. Instead, let the suspect do most of the talking. Experienced interrogators pick up on contradictions and missing links from the narration of events and develop the theme to their advantage. Interrogators should not enter into any argument with the suspect or try to show intellectual superiority, which would lead to the suspect developing defensive mechanisms.

Two primary barriers to entry in the context of interrogation are the suspect's resistance to questioning and establishing rapport with the interrogator. Resistance is the by-product of several factors such as training, country of origin, life experience, personality, commitment to a cause or ideology, deep-rooted feelings about the interrogator and even anger at the manner in which the suspect has been treated since arrest. Once the suspect develops a feeling that information sought by the interrogator would be damaging or incriminating for him personally, and his cooperation with the interrogators would have more adverse consequences for him than his non-cooperation, the intensity of his resistance increases. It is the same with the ideological indoctrination of suspects belonging to extremist outfits like the Islamic State of Iraq and Syria (ISIS) or al-Qaeda who have undergone years of training in their camps and developed radical ideologies dearer to them than even their own lives.

The interrogator's challenge is to manage resistance effectively while systematically working to overcome it. Thus, the interrogator's first task is to identify and deconstruct the suspect's resistance posture and strategies and decide the right strategy. Secondly, the interrogators must confirm that a suspect is actually employing a systematic resistance strategy. Third, they must identify the components of that strategy. Finally, they must devise an effective counterstrategy. On many instances, interrogators require the services of subject matter experts, behavioural scientists, cultural, political, theological and linguistic experts to decipher the resistance meaningfully and identify personality-driven factors or ambiguities during questioning.

Interrogators adopt different tactics to overcome resistance. It usually begins with shrewd questioning. Interrogators assess the possible range of responses the questions may elicit before they are asked and accordingly, they plan and frame an initial question-answer pattern, in which innocuous rapport-building questions are asked. Provocative questions are selectively postponed for later stage. Further, in line with Dr Cialdini's concept of the consistency principle,[94] experienced interrogators pay special attention to avoid creating a situation where the interrogatee has the opportunity to formally assume a resistance posture either by word or deed.

Interrogation experts and authors on interrogation have put together a number of practical measures to overcome resistance and establish rapport with the interrogatees. Some of these suggestions include:

a. The arrest or the shock of capture should be exploited to defuse resistance. If possible, surprise and the maximum amount of mental discomfort should be made use of in order to catch the suspect off balance and to deprive him of initiative. The shock of capture phenomenon is not necessarily limited to the initial point of detention. Every time the detainee is transferred to new surroundings—a new cell, a different wing of the current holding facility, or an entirely new facility—a measure of shock of capture will likely occur. The detainee can be presented with a strange setting, a different routine, new guards and a fresh interrogator.

b. Size up the suspect rapidly and efficiently by analyzing personality, temperament, communication skills and the behavioural baseline of the subject. Using this size up, the interrogator should then determine the approach that will be most useful for this type of suspect.

c. To the suspect, the interrogator should appear sympathetic, sincere, impartial, empathetic and firm, all at the same time. Aubry emphasizes the importance of even the interrogator's entrance, stating that that he must enter with an intangible air, which adds up to confidence, confidence in himself and confidence in his ability to carry out a successful interrogation. But the interrogator should not leave an impression that he is out to get the suspect at all costs, by hook or by crook.

d. Provide an opportunity to the suspect to evaluate the interrogator so as to reach a conclusion or understanding that the interrogator is professional, non-judgmental and knowledgeable. That is why Royal and Schutt write that, "resistance to the disclosure of information is considerably increased if the interrogator is a total stranger, or if something is not done to establish a friendly and trusting attitude on the part of the suspect."

e. Begin the discussion by commenting on a topic of apparent interest to the subject. Do not ask questions that lead the subject to believe that the interrogator is suspicious of him, either by the composition of the question or by the method of asking. Keep conversation informal and easy. Display pleasant emotional responses and avoid unpleasant expressions. In a nutshell, establish confidence and friendliness by talking for a period about everyday subjects.

f. Efforts to establish rapport should appear natural and unassuming so the suspect does not become suspicious of the investigator's motives. In some cases, small talk with the suspect helps to establish rapport, whereas for others, simply establishing the suspect's background information and personal history may be enough to gain his cooperation.

As the interrogation progresses, the interrogator needs to demonstrate his critical abilities such as sensory acuity and flexibility. Sensory acuity is the ability to make rapid and accurate assessments of the developing situation—cause, effect and symbols—during the interrogation. These may be in the form of observable indicators such as a rise in the intensity of stress-induced behaviours when the suspect is confronted with investigative or sensitive questions (e.g., the hideout of a co-accused about which the suspect claims to have no knowledge) and an absence of those same behaviours when the suspect is asked questions about other matters of a non-accusatory nature. Flexibility enables the interrogator to change strategy, tactics, approach, behaviour and the questioning pattern of interrogation in relation to the behaviour and resistance of the suspect. If the suspect becomes reserved and non-cooperative, the right techniques may be used to re-establish rapport.

It has been established that the interrogator's abilities, such as sensory acuity, flexibility, adaptability and speed, are critical factors that decide the success of an interrogation. This can be explained using Boyd's way or his Observe, Orient, Decide and Act (the OODA loop) strategy to elicit information. Developed by military strategists and late US Air Force Colonel John Boyd,[95] OODA is a decision-making model with a recurring cycle of observe – orient – decide – act. Basically, interrogation can be defined as a competition between two decision-making cycles—one by the interrogator and the other by the suspect, in which the successful party is the one that possess and employs the critical elements of adaptability, speed, sensory acuity and flexibility most effectively. According to Boyd, the OODA loop exquisitely captures these elements and provides a unique framework for their systematic, outcome-oriented orchestration. Thus, one must continually observe, orient, decide and act in order to achieve and maintain freedom of action and maximize the chances for survival and success.

In the context of interrogation, observation systematically collects and organizes a suspect's tonality, word choice, gestures, analogies, metaphors and a myriad of other observables in a manner that enables the interrogator to move effectively to the next phase. For example, a suspect who readily answers non-pertinent question and cooperates with the interrogators shows observable changes in posture and speech (verbal and non-verbal indicators) while confronted with pertinent questions. Orientation involves the proper analysis and synthesis of the information gathered during the observation phase. The analysis of the suspect's observable changes when answering pertinent questions opens up the possibility of conscious resistance. Further questioning and analysis and synthesis of the inputs, along with the known background information of the suspect, suggest that the suspect has useful information but refrains from cooperating with the interrogators, thus apprehending personal consequences. On the basis of inputs gathered through observation and orientation, the interrogators must decide an effective course of action. They have various options based on time, tactics and temperament. The interrogation can be prolonged or a new set of interrogators can take up the task or new interrogation techniques can be applied. The final phase, action is the physical manifestation of the decision. Once the action begins, it should be governed by Schwerpunkt (eliciting truth in the shortest possible time). In short, Boyd uses the OODA loop to emphasize that interrogators need to operate with a skilful combination of rapidity, variety, harmony and initiative for success in interrogations.

The success of interrogation should not be measured or determined solely on the basis of a confession or admission obtained from the suspect. Any interrogation solely guided by the goal of confession or led by interrogators with tunnel vision results in bias or contamination, which negate objectivity and truthfulness. The goal of an interrogation should be to gather useful information. Even lies can be as useful in an eventual prosecution as a confession—a professional investigator can procure decisive leads even when a suspect lies, which the suspect does not realize might be useful for investigation or prosecution. Say for example, even the mention of a seemingly random mobile number can be useful, as its Call Data Record (CDR) analysis or monitoring can lead to crucial pieces of evidence, which perhaps may even be more reliable than a half-baked confession by the accused.

The interrogation is an intellectual exercise or a competition between the interrogator and the suspect. For the interrogator, the index of success depends upon the collection of timely, accurate and comprehensive intelligence, information or evidence. For suspects, the intended outcome varies dramatically. While some may fight tooth and nail to stymie the collection of any intelligence or information, others may ultimately provide information in return for specific assurances, actions, privileges, incentives, rewards or treatment such as the promise of an expedited release, enlisting as 'Approver' or a lenient approach towards associates. The suspect's intended outcome will, to a great extent, determine the rate at which intelligence or evidence is offered, as well as both the quality and quantity of such inputs. During this dynamic exchange, both the interrogator and the suspect manage a mosaic of information that can be broadly categorized into three types: what is known (reliable), what is believed to be true (suspected), and what can only be guessed. That is why interrogation is very often described by many as "a carefully controlled exchange of statements of fact and statements of supposition, liberally interspersed with an array of bluffs, feints and ploys." This move-countermove process has been likened to the game of chess, or more appropriately, the ancient Chinese game of Go,[96] where the number of possible combinations of board positions is estimated to be approximately 10 to the 750th power. Fortunately, interrogations, like Go, feature an assortment of recurring situations that, through experience, can be quickly recognized and effectively addressed.

11

Interrogation Techniques for Terrorists and Extremists

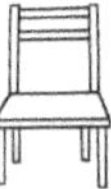

THE NATURE AND OBJECTIVES of interrogations differ depending upon the agencies involved and the nature of suspects. For example, in most criminal investigations, the main focus of the interrogators is to obtain a confession from a suspect, rather than to collect information from possibly, but not necessarily, a cognizant and cooperative suspect. On the other hand, in interrogations of POWs, espionage agents, terrorists or extremists, the main focus is to collect as much strategic input as possible that will be useful to counter or neutralize future plans of the enemy or other hostile elements. Accordingly, agencies adopt different interrogation strategies or techniques to gather the maximum useful information from such categories of interrogatees.

From time immemorial, extreme methods of interrogation have been used to extract information from offenders like political dissidents, extremists or terrorists. For example, in the Soviet Union, Communist rulers adopted inhuman techniques against dissidents and critics of the regime. Aleksandr Solzhenitsyn documented numerous such methods in his classic book *The Gulab Archipelago*. In the 1970s, Great Britain implemented sensory deprivation interrogation methods known as the five techniques[97] against suspected members of the terrorist Irish Republican Army (IRA). The US, during their occupation and operations in countries like Vietnam, Grenada, Panama, Iraq, Kuwait and Afghanistan, followed such methods during the interrogation of detained soldiers or civilians.

In the twenty-first century, when the nations of the world meet their newest enemy—global terrorism—with different moral values, there has been a renewed use of coercive techniques during interrogations, including torture. The post-9/11 period has witnessed a number of Interrogation Centres at places like Guantanamo Bay, Bagram, Abu Ghraib where specialized teams of US interrogators adopt harsh and extreme measures during the interrogation of terror suspects, violating various international covenants and protocols. The special interrogation techniques approved by the US government in April 2003 under the special training program called SERE (Survival, Evasion, Resistance, Escape), which include total isolation, sleep deprivation, forced nudity, sexual humiliation, and water boarding were reminiscent of US soldiers' crude interrogation methods against Vietnamese soldiers and prisoners during the Vietnam war. There has even been a call to legitimize torture or the third degree in the war on terrorism. The Israeli parliament, the Knesset, endorsed the findings the Landau Commission,[98] which justified the use of physical pressure and coercive methods during interrogations and recommended statutory status for such methods. Other major powers like the US, Russia, China are in favour of using such extreme measures in the fight against global terror.

If we pay heed to the post-9/11 debates over guidelines for the interrogation of terrorist suspects, we could easily conclude that coercive and harsh methods are not only effective, but also substantially more useful than non-coercive methods in obtaining actionable intelligence from resistant suspects. Many hold that such methods are essential to gain information from hardcore terrorists about future operations and targets, and to avert major tragedies involving human lives. One such example was the case of Khalid Sheikh Mohammed, the principal architect of the 9/11 attacks on World Trade Centre (WTC) and the right-hand man of Osama Bin Laden. Originally a Pakistani Islamist terrorist, Mohammed, was captured in March 2003 from Rawalpindi, a city in Pakistan, by a combined operation of the CIA and Pakistan's Inter-Services Intelligence (ISI). As he was the CIA's prime catch in their fight against global terrorism, they shifted him to the CIA's secret interrogation camps in Afghanistan and Poland and finally, to Guantanamo Bay detention camp. He was subjected to interrogations using extremely harsh measures, after which the CIA and FBI claimed that Mohammed had not only confessed to his role in around two dozen attacks in different countries, including the 9/11 WTC attack, but also disclosed some listed targets for future attacks. Similarly, the interrogation of David Coleman Headley, the Pakistani-American terrorist and the main architect of the 2008 Mumbai terror attacks, unravelled not only the network and linkages of Lashkar-e-Taiba (LeT) but also the strategies and plans of al-Qaeda and other terrorist groups in different countries.

Highlighting these success stories, the US, which is at the forefront of the fight against global terrorism, has adopted more such coercive methods of interrogation. Thus, the CIA manual underscores that, "the coercive methods are designed not only to exploit the resistant source's internal conflicts and induce him to wrestle with himself but also to bring a superior outside force to bear upon the subject's resistance." The chief coercive techniques they use for interrogation include: arrest, detention, deprivation of sensory stimuli through solitary confinement or similar methods, threats and fear, debility, pain, heightened suggestibility and hypnosis, narcosis (use of drugs) and induced regression. However, the US Senate Report (Senate Select Committee on Intelligence, 2014) on the CIA's enhanced interrogation strategies deemed "these techniques as ineffective at acquiring intelligence and ultimately damaged the country's standing in the world."

The question of how useful coercive techniques are in the interrogation of terrorists or extremists has been widely discussed among law enforcers, criminologists and researchers. Of course, there are mixed responses, depending upon a variety of factors such as the context of the detention of the suspect, his or her personality, training, commitment and the skills of interrogators. Researchers have found that harsh and coercive techniques damage the value and reliability of the information generated (Gudjonsson, 2003), create significant negative effects on mental health of the interrogatee leading to anxiety, depression, cognitive disturbances, distortions, obsessive thoughts, paranoia and psychosis (Metzner and Fellner, 2010) and increase resistance (Dreher, Gassebner and Siemers, 2010).[99] In short, coercive techniques have many immediate, medium-term, and long-term negative effects. They breach all of the most basic moral codes of psychologists and psychiatrists, contravene international law and have no empirical basis or evidence for being effective.

As the main focus of strategic interrogation is to generate intelligence or information about the structure, organization, membership, strategy/tactics, communication, finances and targets of terrorist organizations or hostile elements, intelligence agencies have explored other potential methods of interrogation. One such method is the Observing Rapport-Based Interpersonal Techniques (ORBIT), a model developed on the basis of two known areas on the social spectrum. The first one is therapeutic interventions or Motivational Interviewing (MI), originally derived from approaches used with substance users to get them out of the menacing influence of drugs and psychotropic substances. The second one is the different aspects of the Interpersonal Behavioural Circle (IBC) relating to the interpersonal patterns associated with various psychological disorders. In the case of MI, interrogators use various factors such as acceptance, empathy, adaptation, evocation and autonomy—depending upon the nature of the suspect. While expressing empathy with the suspect, interrogators point out the discrepancies or contradictions in the suspect's approach, such as his or her blind faith in certain ideologies or convictions. They avoid argumentation and use the suspect's resistance to help build his motivation to cooperate with the interrogators. Just like a therapist tries to help a drug addict out of his or her dream world of drugs, the interrogators try to elicit information from a terror suspect by highlighting the hollowness of their ideology or activities.

In the case of IBC, interrogators use a conducive communication style (adaptive) and avoid a maladaptive or authoritative style of demanding, or a dogmatic approach. Such an adaptive communication style, coupled with versatility, helps interrogators reduce the suspect's various counterinterrogation tactics or defence mechanisms, which may include: pretending lack of knowledge or memory, remaining silent, making monosyllabic responses, retracting statements. A team of experts from Liverpool University, UK, who conducted detailed research[100] on the ORBIT model, found that this method is useful for the interrogation of terrorists and generation of enhanced intelligence or information from such suspects. As part of the research, they analyzed a large data set of terrorist interrogations, through audio and video footage, of over 180 convicted suspects, including international terrorists, domestic terrorists and paramilitary terrorists.

In war, the interrogation of enemy soldiers and POWs is of considerable significance for generating tactical or military intelligence. Such foreknowledge about the enemy, as rightly observed by Sun Tzu, the ancient Chinese strategist and military writer of fifth century BC, is not restricted to the mere strength of the enemy forces but includes other information about the enemy such as their economy, industrial secrets, modern weaponry, advancements in technology and cyberspace. Captured enemy soldiers are the best sources to cater such vital intelligence thus, they are subjected to interrogations using all available means in order to collect such tactical and strategic intelligence. On many instances, overenthusiastic interrogators violate the clauses of the Geneva Convention or other protocols on the rights and privileges of POWs. Such strategies have been used during the interrogation of civilian-detainees of hostile countries or detained terrorists or non-state actors.

In the fight against global terrorism, police and other law enforcement agencies adopt different approaches for terrorism-related interrogations. One common approach is to use the services of highly educated and specially trained personnel in counterterrorism squads, who have expertise or experience in the fields of interrogation and hostage negotiation. But, given the psychological and behavioural complexity of interrogations in general, and the sensitivity of terrorism related interrogations in particular, ad-hoc arrangements need to be discouraged. Instead, better trained and dedicated interrogators should be deployed for sensitive assignments. Another approach is the use of non-conventional interrogation techniques in the case of terror-suspects with different cultural or linguistic backgrounds. In *The Anguish of Surrender*,[101] Ulrich Straus described how American interrogators had successfully used this technique in the interrogation of Japanese POWs during the Second World War. The POWs who remained entirely uncooperative, sullen and arrogant with the interrogators very often freely interacted with the interrogators when the interrogators spent more time with them. Moreover, in the aftermath of such interactions, the POWs reacted favourably to certain facilities extended by the interrogators, such as better medical treatment or ample food. By exploiting such behaviour, the US interrogators could successfully gather useful tactical and military intelligence from those POWs.

For terrorists or non-state actors, their differences in cultural background can be explored through trial and error for fruitful interrogations. On the other hand, cultural and linguistic similarities of the suspects with the interrogators have the added advantage for the interrogators to establish good rapport with them. For example, a vast number of Pakistani citizens who trace their roots to India have a cultural and linguistic familiarity with people in India. These factors could be exploited during the interrogation of suspects from that country. Moreover, the global war on terrorism contains seeds of Samuel Huntington's *Clash of Civilizations*,[102] in which rivals exploit cultural and ideological diversities as well as similarities. In such scenarios, instead of adhering to conventions or preconceptions, interrogators should adopt a rational approach and present an apparently logical explanation or rationalization for the suspect to capitulate and cooperate with the interrogators. This approach is almost along the lines of Dr Robert Cialdini's Principle of Consistency, which holds that when a person faces interpersonal pressure, he or she may behave in a manner consistent with what they have said or done previously. This could be illustrated by a simple example:

Interrogator: We both agree that God would condemn acts that result in the killing of innocent people, especially women and children. If you truly believe in God as you have said, you tell me about the next target of ISIS so that you and I, two believers in God, can work together to avert the death of so many innocent people.[103]

Such an approach, commonly known as circular logic, works well with less-hardened and highly religious or fundamentalist suspects.

Beyond the models of interrogation, an essential requirement for interrogators is scientific and technical expertise and an extensive technological vocabulary, as many terrorist groups excel in the areas of science, technology and cybernetics. Basically, the primary task of interrogators is to identify and understand the centres of gravity of terrorism, which as rightly conceptualized by Carl von Clausewitz,[104] are "the hub of all power and movement on which everything depends." In the context of the ongoing war against terrorism, the centres of gravity of terrorism include the ability to communicate, move, transport items, secure a safe haven, obtain financial support and develop expertise in weapons and explosives. Therefore, interrogators must approach detainees with sufficient technical competence and understanding so as to elicit the required inputs from them.

Let us discuss a few of these centres of gravity of terrorist operations. The information revolution has opened up an unprecedented array of options for all, including terrorists, for speedy communication across the globe. Cellular phones with fake Subscriber Identity Modules (SIM), instant messaging, chat rooms and steganography have been extensively used by terrorist groups in planning and staging attacks. For example, ISIS has been observed to be using such digitalized communication channels for the dissemination of their ideology, the recruitment of members and planning attacks or special operations. As such groups rely heavily on sophisticated means of covert and secure communication channels for their various operations in different countries, it becomes critical for an interrogator to possess the requisite technical expertise to effectively exploit a terror-detainee's knowledge in these areas. It is the same with terror-financing and allied activities. The 9/11 Commission Report of the National Commission on Terrorist Attacks upon the United States revealed that al-Qaeda operatives spent between $400,000 and $500,000 to plan and conduct the attacks. The crucial question was how they had mobilized such huge sum and clandestinely moved them from different countries to the coffers of al-Qaeda, virtually surpassing normal banking or other financial channels. It has been now established that terrorist organizations use both cutting-edge technology and ancient means of financing such as Hawala, the underground, trust-based banking system that facilitates the movement of money without a trailing record of transactions. With the introduction of cryptocurrency and its wide application in financial transactions, terrorists and drug syndicates have laid their hands on such means to funnel illegal finances. Given the complexity of global finance, it is exceedingly difficult to identify the funding that supports terrorism. An interrogator who lacks an understanding of how money moves across international boundaries; how currencies are transformed into digital equivalents; the nature of national and international reporting requirements on transactions; constantly evolving money laundering schemes and the system of Hawala, will have a limited ability to leverage the potential intelligence of a well-placed, knowledgeable suspect or detainee. As the global financial sector rapidly changes through innovative mechanisms and procedures for money transfer and investment across the globe that surpass financial and trade barriers, terror-outfits and radical organizations will definitely utilize them for clandestine transactions. Thus, law enforcement agencies and their specialized groups can combat these challenges only by overcoming the technical and knowledge barriers that confront them during their conflict with terrorist and extremist outfits.

12

Interrogation Approaches and Techniques

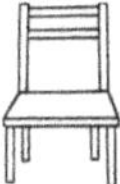

IN ANY INTERROGATION, THE methods and techniques used depend on certain basic factors such as the suspect, the nature of offense, the suspect's degree of implication and participation in the crime, the facts pertinent to his or her apprehension. Thus, Aubry correctly notes, "the approach should be adapted to the type, character, and general background of the person being interrogated; the known facts, events and incidents of the crime which has been committed; and the type, kind, nature and extent of the physical evidence available."[105] Based on his hypothesis, he broadly classified these approaches as a) direct approach, which is most suitable in cases where the guilt of the subject is certain, or reasonably certain, b) indirect approach, suitable in cases where the degree of guilt is indicated with something less than reasonable certitude, c) emotional approach, which depends on the personal qualities of the suspect such as his or her religious beliefs or other emotional factors and d) subterfuge, considered to be a very effective approach but should only be used if the guilt of the suspect is reasonably certain and standard approaches have been tried and have failed.

Aubry lists several general interrogation techniques which include: demolishing the suspect's resistance by establishing motive, premeditation, propensity to commit the crime, hammering away at the suspect persistently to get the truth and nibbling off little pieces of the interrogation cake, instead of concentrating on crumbs, but not biting off pieces too big to chew. Rather than being distracted by the suspect's initial disclosures, interrogators should strive to elicit the whole truth or all the facts connected with the crime or incident.

Some specific interrogation techniques that Aubry highlights are:

a. Singleness of purpose: This emphasizes concentrating on the sole aim of obtaining a confession or eliciting the maximum truth from the suspect.

b. Businesslike attitude: The degree of success of an interrogation is determined by the nature of the feelings, beliefs and values that the interrogator projects during the encounter with the suspect. The entire process should be like a business deal between a smart businessman and a cooperative customer. This reminds us of Hans Gross' definition of a good interrogator.

c. Calm and matter-of-fact: The interrogator should demonstrate sound presence of mind throughout the interrogation and his or her focus should be to get concrete evidence or collect useful intelligence.

d. Don't be shocked, whatever the provocation: Interrogators should not lose their temper, nor fall into the trap of provocation by the suspect.

e. Let the suspect tell his or her story: Usually, the interrogation begins with open-ended questions or free narration, which allow the interrogators to assess the suspect's approach towards them.

f. Let the suspect tell a few lies: Invariably, a suspect's disclosures might be truthful, semi-truthful or total lies. Interrogators can successfully exploit the common saying, "To hide one lie, a thousand lies are needed."

g. A waste of your time and mine: This technique is useful when the suspect continues to show signs of resistance and does not cooperate with the interrogators, who should then indicate that they would be forced to adopt other approaches and methods.

h. You're just hurting your loved ones: Interrogators can send a clear message to the suspect that by not cooperating with them, he or she is engaged in self-destructive behaviour that would adversely affect their near and dear ones.

i. Proven lies, so tell the truth: Once the lies are established, the suspect has no other alternative but to tell the truth. The common dictum is, "Every lie we tell incurs a debt to the truth. Sooner or later, that debt is paid."

j. Hammer at right and wrong: A warning to the effect that fair and bad things may occur.

k. How about your conscience? Reminding suspects of one's obligations to do the right things in life.

l. Establishing motives: Interrogators give an indication that a suspect's motives have been established—then why should he or she refuse to admit to the crime or offense?

m. Hate to be in your shoes: Interrogators create an impression that the suspect is really in a difficult and complex situation.

n. Things look awfully bad for you: A technique to highlight the real plight of the suspect or accused.

o. Confusion by false incidents: An attempt to minimize or dilute the offense.

p. Confession of co-defendant: Just like the technique of 'bhed' in *Chanakya Niti*, this technique is meant to create differences among suspects and extract specific inputs.

q. The genuine confession: Highlights the positives of confession.

Royal and Schutt have established an overarching schema of techniques for a successful interrogation. According to them, an interrogator's primary task is to undermine the accused's confidence in success by demonstrating the futility of his or her position and "blocking all non-cooperative avenues of escape." Interrogators must detect deception, overcome alibis and emphasize the quality and quantity of incriminating evidence against the suspect. Secondly, they may offer the accused a mutually acceptable solution after convincing him that he is confronted with a personal emergency from which he cannot easily escape or find a way out—the only option would be to accept the proposal of the interrogators, which would result in less unpleasantness than any of the other solutions. The third step is to increase the likelihood of the accused's confession when the interrogators demonstrate objectivity, sympathy and sincerity. In such a case, the suspect would be mentally prepared to surrender and leave his destiny in the hands of the interrogators. The next phase is to observe the first signs of the accused positively responding to the interrogator's suggestions. Then the interrogator should begin to diminish other confession inhibiting factors and provide incentives for the suspect to confess through theme development, as suggested by the Reid technique. Finally, when the suspect submits and agrees to cooperate, the offered gain should be immediately consolidated and rendered as irreversible as possible. In some cases, a written confession statement is recorded.

On a closer analysis, we find that some of the common techniques adopted by interrogators include:

a. Demonstration of empathy, kindness, helpfulness and friendliness
b. Extenuation or mitigation of crime
c. Shifting the blame on others
d. Hot-cold treatment
e. Minimizing the consequences of the offense
f. Bluffing
g. A businesslike approach
h. Pretence of physical evidence
i. Appeals to decency and honour

Accordingly, interrogators have to play different roles such as an experienced schoolmaster, humane philosopher, philanthropist, psychological counsellor, helpful colleague, rational lawyer, regimented personnel, bluff master, and of course, a talented and dynamic business executive or representative.

Regardless of their background or personality, suspects try to reduce their anxiety and tension through body movements or other physical activities—which work by displacement and distraction. Their mind will simultaneously attempt to reduce anxiety through a series of hypothetical constructs called Defence Mechanisms (DMs). Interrogation is successful only if the suspect's DMs are made inoperative or inactive. Psychologists like Anna Freud have extensively studied DMs, which are basic human instincts to defend ourselves from unpleasant events, actions or thoughts. Such psychological strategies enable people to keep distance between themselves and threats or unwanted feelings, such as guilt or shame. Suspects use various DMs to cover up the crime or offense and interrogators can elicit the truth only by breaking the chain of these mechanisms.

Successful interrogators adopt various strategies to defeat these mechanisms. Rationalization, Projection and Minimization, commonly known as RPM, is the best technique to make DMs inactive or inoperative. Rationalization is the act of re-describing what a person did in such a way as to avoid any responsibility for the consequences of his behaviour. It is the business of the interrogator to provide the right rationalization at the right time. Here, too, the importance of understanding the interrogatee is evident—the right rationalization must be reason that is tailored to the suspect's personality. In Projection, interrogators attribute the suspect's criminal behaviour to someone else and create an impression that the criminal action was not his or her own fault. With Minimization, interrogators reduce the suspect's role in the crime or the seriousness of the offense. At a fundamental level, the true challenge for the interrogator is to make it as difficult as possible for the suspect to resist or to make it as easy as possible for him or her to cooperate.

Let us practically examine RPM through a simulated interrogation of a 47-year-old woman, the primary accused of the alleged Cyanide Murders of 6 people that occurred in a southern state in India over a span of 14 years, from 2002-2016. The accused was born in a lower middle class farmer's family in a remote village. As her father did not have the finances to support her college education, she, a below average student, studied in a parallel college and obtained an education in commerce. She married a middle-class businessman whose parents were teachers. In the husband's house, she was like a fish out of water, with a dominating mother-in law, a father-in-law who kept absolute control of all properties and estates and a servile husband more loyal and obedient to his parents than his wife. Depressed and frustrated, and with an inferiority complex, the woman procured fake credentials and pretended to be a highly qualified professional working as faculty in a nearby reputed engineering institution. Her daily visits to the institution as a part of her profession had ignited her ambitions. The investigators found that her insatiable zest for power, position, authority, money, better sex, pleasures and social status led her to murder the six people, including her husband, mother-in law, father-in law and other relatives. Thus, police investigators have compared her with John Bodkin Adams[106] and Dr Harold Shipman[107] while psychoanalysts and criminologists who studied her psychic factors and behavioural aberrations were of the view that her mental agony and their desire for pleasure and luxuries made her a serial killer, almost along the lines of Jeremy Bentham's concept of pleasure and pain.[108]

In order to use the RPM techniques, or for that matter, any other technique, interrogators need to obtain a detailed factual analysis of the suspect that incorporates his or her biosocial profile and facts connected with the crime. Equally important is to correctly judge the suspect's emotions and feelings during interrogation. For example, during the interrogation of the accused woman in the case above, she would definitely narrate her trials and tribulations in the husband's house. By developing a theme based on such facts and by empathizing with her, the interrogators can comment that they knew well how difficult her life was in that house (Rationalization). When she continues to narrate such bitter experiences in the house, whether true or deceptive, the interrogators can try to console her, affirming that such a cruel fate awaited many poor girls married into rich or affluent families (Projection). Another possible theme for Projection could be her husband, who instead of defending his wife, remained a silent spectator to the humiliation and sufferings of his wife. The interrogator can say that "tragedies" like what happened in her life were natural in such circumstances (Minimization). Such tactics would help to lessen the burden of offense in her mind. Once the interrogators observe that such techniques have had a positive impact on her, their next move is to motivate or persuade her to admit or confess her guilt, which they should present as the best option before her.

When using RPM or similar techniques in interrogation, interrogators should adhere to some fundamental principles. These techniques should be natural and spontaneous, and the themes or comments developed by the interrogators should be compatible with the nature of the offense or the background of the suspect. Secondly, these techniques should be used at the right time and in the right manner so as to establish better rapport with the suspect, ultimately leading to his or her admission or confession of the crime. Thirdly, interrogators need to use magic words or statements that create a decisive impact on the suspect's approach. For example, in the Cyanide Murders above, terms such as "tragedy" or "happenings" can be used instead of "murders" in order to lessen the gravity of the crime. Similar words like "accident," "sudden provocation," "misjudgement," "self-defence" or "mishaps" can be used to describe serious offenses like homicide, murder, and grievous hurt. This leads us to two popular styles of interrogation namely, feather touch style and sledge hammer style. As the name indicates, in feather touch style, interrogators use such magic words or statements to get into the suspect's mind and prompt him or her to admit the offense. On the other hand, in sledge hammer style, they use harsh words, expressions or gestures that create fear, panic or anxiety in the mind of the suspect, leading to confession.

Often, in contrast to Minimization, Maximization techniques are used in the case of vulnerable or first-time offenders. In this technique, interrogators exaggerate or magnify the crime or offense. For example, in a theft case, interrogators might present the amount of stolen money as ₹50 lakhs instead of the actual ₹5 lakhs or in an assault case, they describe the victim who suffered a simple hurt as one inflicted with a grievous hurt and struggling with life and death in the hospital bed. Here, interrogators are exploiting the fear that is created in the mind of vulnerable suspects due to the seriousness of the crime.

Deflation and Inflation of the Ego: These techniques are commonly used with emotional and sensitive suspects involved in sensational cases. In Deflation, interrogators consciously try to belittle the achievements, skills or reputation of the suspect by using statements or expressions to deflate him or her. For example, interrogators can systematically try to belittle the technical skills and expertise of a young suspect involved in a serious explosion and hailed in their circles as a genius in making complex explosive devices—he or she would ultimately burst, unable to withstand the psychological humiliation.

Inflation the opposite of deflation, in which the skills or achievements of the high-profile suspect are exaggerated in such a manner to give him or her a halo or a superhuman image, followed by a series of questions about how such a great hero could have fallen from grace by committing the offense. The suspect's inflated ego works to the advantage of the interrogators. Inflation has been successfully used in breaking a number of high-profile suspects involved in sensational cases.

In sensational cases built on circumstantial evidence, investigators use the technique of fair and reasonable assurance to the suspect least involved in the offense. They explain to the suspect, in simple terms, how a confession would help him or her to get a lesser punishment or how it would help them to become 'approver' in the case. Though such techniques are meant to strengthen prosecution evidence in sensational cases and ensure the conviction of real culprits, investigators guided by vested interests misuse such techniques in many cases to implicate innocent persons.

To neutralize DMs, interrogators should be in a position to correctly assess the suspect's emotions and feelings during interrogation. In many instances, interrogator's make the wrong assessment about the emotions or feelings of the suspects. For example, sometimes frustration is misjudged as anger or guilt, concern as frustration or desperation, depression as fear or apprehension and confusion as non-cooperation. When the suspect expresses mixed feelings or emotions, making the right assessment becomes more arduous. Improper or incorrect assessment of the suspect's emotions incapacitate the interrogators from applying the right responses and approach for the suspect. They would not be able to apply any counter-DMs nor establish proper rapport with the suspect. An interrogator's overdependence on folklore or hackneyed concepts of human behaviour or dynamics is the main factor that contributes to such improper or incorrect assessment of a suspect's feelings.

Wrong assessments of a suspect's emotions very often lead to wrong assumptions, presumptions and preconceived theories about suspects and the offense, which can derail of the entire interrogation. Sometimes interrogators with a preconceived approach play up such emotions, prompting the suspect to make false or fake confessions.

The crucial question is, how do interrogators reach the correct assessment of the suspect's emotions? First and foremost, there is no golden rule on such themes, as the human mind and behaviour are so complex and varied that no common scale can be used to assess feelings across different situations. However, interrogators well versed in a myriad of emotions and feelings of different types of suspects during the different processes and phases of interrogation do well in properly assessing such emotions. Naturally, experience matters a lot. Familiarity with and a better understanding of various verbal and non-verbal responses of suspects, as we discussed earlier, have an added advantage in such matters.

Experienced interrogators adopt a number of practical tips to break suspects and elicit the truth. One common technique is that they consciously create an impression that there is concrete evidence against the suspect. They act convincingly that confession or admission is immaterial but that as investigators with a humane approach, they can do their best to help him or her. An interrogator's actions such as perusing case files or records while the suspect is replying to crucial questions would give more credence to this technique. In offenses committed by more than one person, interrogators create an impression that the suspect's accomplices have already confessed and implicated him or her as the major player in the crime.

With high-profile suspects, interrogators stir up their emotions by highlighting their status and background and their present plight and helplessness in contrast. They sympathize with the suspect, point out his or her tension and nervousness and make an appeal to the suspect to confess the crime so that his or her close relations, friends and colleagues can be saved from the present ordeal. Sometimes, interrogators prompt the suspect's relations and friends to persuade him or her to tell the truth. When such techniques fail, interrogators switch over to sledge hammer style and condemn the suspect, claiming that he or she would never change as his or her accomplices are also the birds of the same feather flock together or that a crow can never turn white even after many baths. Friend and Enemy method is another common technique in interrogation. German interrogators had widely used this technique during the interrogation of British agents or POWs during World War II. In this technique, one interrogator is cruel and harsh to the suspect and even threatens torture if the suspect's replies are not satisfactory. On the other hand, another interrogator appears scholarly and humane and adopts a schoolmaster type approach to slowly develop rapport with the suspect.

The CIA's KUBARK Counterintelligence Interrogation Manual, 1963 and the Field Manuel (FM-34-52) Intelligence interrogation[109] published by the US Army in 1992 and intended for use by CIA interrogators as well as military intelligence personnel, contain a number of techniques used during the interrogation of POWs or detained terrorists. Some of the major techniques include:

Direct approach: This approach involves the straightforward questioning of the POW or detainee without concealing the interrogator's purpose or using deception of any kind, especially when the prisoner is cooperative. The shock of detention acts as the motivating factor for the interrogatee to cooperate.

Incentive-based techniques: The incentive approach rewards the detainee for his or her cooperation. Normally, interrogators would not withhold anything the prisoner is entitled to receive by right under the Geneva Conventions, but they may withhold privileges such as better food or an opportunity to communicate with family. Whether the use of such "privileges" or "entitlements" is appropriate under the Geneva Conventions may depend on the circumstances. For example, one US court found that depriving POWs any opportunity at all to communicate with the outside world amounted to torture.

Emotional love-hate technique: Using the emotional approach, an interrogator seeks to exploit the detainee's emotions in order to override his rationale for resisting. The interrogator makes use of the love the detainee feels toward his family, homeland, comrades to devise an effective incentive, such as communication or promised reunification with his family, a quicker end to the war to save his comrades' lives, and so forth.

Fear up harsh or mild: The aim of the increased fear up harsh technique is to convince the detainee who appears to be hiding something that he does indeed have something to fear (not necessarily from the interrogator) and that he has no option but to cooperate. The interrogator will behave in a heavy, overpowering manner, using a loud and threatening voice.

Reduced fear: The decreased fear down approach is used primarily on a detainee who is already in a state of fear. The technique involves calming the subject and convincing him that he will be properly and humanely treated, or that he is safer in captivity than in combat.

Pride and ego up approach: Through this technique, interrogators elicit sensitive information from the suspect using the trick of flattery or abuse. The pride and ego up variation is used on detainees who feel inferior, especially low-ranking personnel or junior grade officers, who might respond to the opportunity to demonstrate their intellect or importance. The interrogator speaks as if he is very impressed with the suspect's accomplishments, engendering positive feelings in detainee that he is finally getting the recognition he deserves. He may reveal pertinent information in order to solicit more laudatory comments from the interrogator.

Pride and ego down approach: In this technique, interrogators exploit a detainee's sense of inferiority by attacking his personal worth, criticizing his loyalty, intelligence, abilities, technical competence, leadership qualities, slovenly appearance or any other perceived weakness. The interrogator uses a sarcastic, caustic tone of voice to express distaste or disgust. If the tactic works, the detainee will become defensive and try to prove the interrogator wrong. In his attempt to vindicate his pride, he will usually, involuntarily, provide pertinent information.

Futility approach: The futility approach is used to exploit the doubts and misgivings already in the detainee's mind to make him believe that it is useless to resist the interrogation. By making the situation appear hopeless, the interrogator allows the source to rationalize his cooperation.

We know all: The 'we know all' approach involves making a detainee believe that the interrogator already knows everything about him. Based on compiled and collated data on the detainee and his unit, interrogators ask questions to which they already know the answer. When the detainee refuses to answer or provides an incomplete or false response, the interrogator himself supplies the correct answer. Thus, the interrogator tries to convince the detainee that all information is already known, so he may as well cooperate.

Establish your identity: In the establish your identity approach, the interrogator insists that the detainee has been identified as an infamous criminal who is merely posing as someone else to avoid punishment. The source may be tricked into giving detailed information about his unit to establish or substantiate his true identity and refute the interrogator's allegations.

Repetition: The interrogator may repeat the same question several times in order to get a hostile suspect to cooperate. The suspect becomes bored with the repetition and may give more complete and candid answers simply to gain relief from the monotony. Taken to extremes, for example during prolonged interrogations, it might be said to induce mental suffering.

File and dossier: The file and dossier approach is a variation of the we know all approach, but uses a prop. Prior to the session, the interrogator prepares a dossier containing all available information obtained from records and documents concerning the subject or his organization, possibly padding it with extra paper to create the illusion that it contains much more information than is really there. The interrogator confronts the subject with the dossier, exploiting the known facts about him to convince him that resistance would be futile.

Rapid fire: The rapid-fire approach is a psychological ploy "based upon the principles that everyone likes to be heard when he speaks, and it is confusing to be interrupted in mid-sentence with an unrelated question." One or two interrogators ask a series of questions without allowing the subject time to answer completely before the next question is asked. The subject may become confused and contradict himself, which the interrogator can exploit by confronting the subject with the inconsistencies. He may reveal more than he intends in attempting to clarify his answers.

Silence: The silence approach involves an interrogator who says nothing to the source but "looks him squarely in the eye, preferably with a slight smile on his face," in an effort to make the subject nervous and force him to break eye contact first. The subject may begin to talk or ask questions to break the tension. Ali

Soufan, FBI interrogator, successfully used this technique during the interrogation of Ahmad Mohammad al-Badawi,, an al-Qaeda operative involved in the USS Cole bombing.

Ivan is a dope: It is a non-coercive technique in which the detainee's agency or organization is projected in a bad light that it is least concerned about the fate or welfare of its personnel or agents. The interrogator sells the interrogatee an idea that unlike his agency, he (the interrogator) and his organization are truly concerned about his welfare. Perhaps the best example is the interrogation of Houssine Kherchtou, the al-Qaeda leader. FBI interrogators, citing the al-Qaeda's refusal to pay for a Caesarean section for Kherchtou's wife, created an impression that al-Qaeda is least interested in the welfare of its operatives or their suffering family members.

Mutt and Jeff routine or good cop, bad cop: This works best with women, juveniles and timid suspects. While one interrogator plays the role of an angry, aggressive cop using intimidatory and abusive language and expressions, the other interrogator presents himself as a saviour of the interrogatee with polished words and gentle behaviour.

Alice in Wonderland or the power of applied confusion: The aim of the Alice in Wonderland or confusion technique is to confound the expectations and conditioned reactions of the interrogatee. It is designed not only to obliterate a suspect's sense of predictability or continuity and logic, but to replace it with confusion. As the process continues, the subject tries to make sense of the situation, which becomes mentally intolerable. The result is that he is likely to make significant admissions or even to pour out his whole story.

These approaches, by and large, fulfil the provisions of the Geneva Conventions on the rights and privileges of POWs. But, in the aftermath of 9/11 and USA's organized fight against global terrorism, US agencies, notably the CIA, adopted Enhanced Interrogation Techniques, which in many respects deviated from the guidelines of the Geneva Conventions and many other United Nations conventions and protocols on human rights and the charter of duties of law enforcement personnel. Some of these techniques are:

Isolation: The detainee is isolated from other detainees and kept in solitary cells for a prolonged period. It is considered an exceptional technique, and its extensive use could fall under torture or cruel, inhuman and degrading treatment under the UN Charter.

Sleep deprivation: It is an age-old method for physically weakening the subject. However, the CIA manual recommends sleep disruption as a more effective method of coercion. Sometimes, sleep adjustment is also used. The detainee's ordinary sleep schedule is disturbed for example, by reversing the sleep cycles from night to day, but without depriving the detainee of sleep. The method likely induces a feeling of disorientation similar to jet lag. Such techniques were extensively used during the interrogation of 9/11 detainees in the CIA's Guantanamo and Abu Ghraib interrogation camps.

Sensory deprivation: As per the CIA manual, it is a byproduct of solitary confinement and isolation. Artificially limiting the extent to which a person is able to sense his environment has been found to induce stress and when taken to the extreme, can cause hallucinations and delusions. According to one expert, "It is obvious that inner factors in the mind tend to be projected outward, that some of the mind's activity which is usually reality-bound becomes free to turn to phantasy and ultimately to hallucination and delusion."

Environmental manipulation: This method involves alteration of the environment to create moderate discomfort, by adjusting the room's temperature or introducing an unpleasant smell, without creating conditions that would injure the detainee. Purposeful exposure of POWs to temperature extremes for interrogation purposes has been found to be ill-treatment under the 1929 Geneva Conventions.

Dietary manipulation: This technique involves changing the diet of a detainee, but not in such a way as to deprive him of food or water, affect his health or interfere with his religious practices. The objective is probably to disorient the detainee by upsetting his regular routine.

Change of scenery down: For this technique, the interrogator removes the detainee from the standard interrogation setting to one that may be less comfortable but would not constitute a substantial change in environmental quality. The purpose of a change of scenery is to throw the detainee psychologically off balance.

Presence of military working dogs: The presence of military dogs that does not directly threaten or endanger the detainee was suggested as a method to create anxiety but not terror or mental trauma.

Removal of all comfort items, including religious items: This technique is a harsher version of the removal of incentives. The removal of religious items could entail a violation of Geneva Convention articles.

Forced grooming: Forced grooming includes shaving the detainee's hair or beard to outrage his human dignity or religious rights.

Use of scenarios designed to convince the detainee that death or severely painful consequences are imminent: This technique was listed as a Category III technique that could only be used to interrogate the most uncooperative detainees at Guantanamo, with the approval of the Commanding General. Category III techniques also included exposure to cold weather or water and "the use of a wet towel and dripping water to induce a feeling of suffocation."

The memoirs of Ali Soufan,[110] one of the leading interrogators of the FBI who successfully interrogated a number of prominent al-Qaeda leaders including the perpetrators of the 9/11 attacks, shed light on various techniques of interrogation. According to him, the most potent weapon interrogators can use against ideologically committed cadres of outfits like al-Qaeda is knowledge. In the words of Ali Soufan, "Our greatest successes against al-Qaeda have come when we understood how they recruited, brainwashed, and operated, and used our knowledge to outwit and defeat them. Our failures have come when we instead let ourselves be guided by ignorance, fear, and brutality. It's the difference between acting out of fear and acting out of knowledge."[111]

Ali Soufan's experience tells us that one of the main points of influence on a detainee is the impression he has of the evidence against him. Thus, an interrogator needs to do a lot of homework and collect as much information as possible about the detainee and become an expert in every detail. He then uses that knowledge to impress upon the detainee that everything about him is known and any lie would be easily detected. For example, as mentioned before in this chapter, in the case of Kherchtou, the al-Qaeda leader who trained the outfit's operatives in aircraft operations, information on al-Qaeda's refusal to pay for a Caesarean section for his wife, enabled interrogators to exploit his deep frustration and anguish against the outfit. With Ali Hamsa Ahmad Suliman al-Bahlul, Bin Laden's secretary and propagandist, interrogators played on intelligence about his commitment to al-Qaeda and his religious knowledge. And with Mohammad Abdel Karim al Ghezali, one of the founders of al-Qaeda in the Arabian Peninsula, it was his childhood feelings toward his brother that exposed him.

On the contrary, efforts to break the detainee into compliance without knowing anything about him or the level of his involvement can have disastrous consequences. In such a scenario, interrogators are unable to assess whether the information given by the detainee is accurate, pointless or false. Moreover, terror outfits like al-Qaeda train their operatives to come up with false narratives. The Manchester Manual of al-Qaeda advised operatives to admit things they knew the interrogator knew, giving the impression that they were cooperating, while withholding the real truth and any new information.

Soufan holds that the shock of capture and detention and isolation from his support base, very often, led the detainee to desire interaction with someone reliable and dependable. The interrogator turns this mental condition to his advantage by becoming the one person the detainee can talk to and who listens to what he has to say. He uses this to encourage the detainee to open up. As the interrogator is the person speaking to and listening to the detainee, a relationship is built—and the detainee doesn't want to jeopardize it.

Perhaps the best example for this approach, according to Soufan, was the interrogation of Abu Zubaydah. He is a Saudi citizen suspected to be involved in training al-Qaeda operatives at Khaldun training camp in Afghanistan. He was captured in Pakistan in 2002 and sent to the US interrogation base in Thailand. An FBI team comprising Ali Soufan and Steve Gaudin initially interrogated him in Thailand using traditional interrogation methods. Soufan had all the background information about Zubaydah and on their first meeting in the hospital, called him Hani, his mother's nickname for Zubaydah when he was a child. This technique made him cooperate with the interrogation. As he was in a hospital bed in serious condition, Soufan placed blocks of ice on his lips to give him some liquid, and Steve cleaned him up after he soiled himself. He was saved from his death bed and subsequently disclosed all about Khalid Sheikh Mohammed Al Mukhtar, the mastermind of the 9/11 attacks, and that American Jose Padilla[112] had wanted to use a dirty bomb in a terror attack. Subsequently, a CIA team that interrogated him to extract more sensitive actionable intelligence by using Enhanced Interrogation

Techniques failed to elicit any additional inputs as Zubaydah did not cooperate with them. But he continued to cooperate with the FBI team and its members like Soufan whose traditional interrogation techniques had created a positive impression in his mind.

Soufan narrates a few episodes demonstrating how simple techniques can corner trained terrorists during interrogation. For example, during the interrogation of Abu Jindal al Nasser al Bahri (Osama Bin Laden's former chief bodyguard), interrogators could exploit his religious and ideological sentiments by showing him the headlines of a Yemeni newspaper that talked about 200 Yemenis being killed in the WTC attack. Jandal, originally from Yemen, took the attack as something contrary to his deep religious faith and convictions and had no qualms to denounce the act and blame the perpetrators of the crime. But when the interrogation progressed, he had to identify and admit that the perpetrators who were al-Qaeda operatives, some of them with long-standing associations with him.

The presence of a co-interrogator who never opens his mouth but occasionally scribbles something on a pad and passes it to the other interrogator is a technique that got Jamal Ahmad Mohammad Al-Badawi (the terrorist behind the 2000 attack on the USS Cole) into mental doldrums. The interrogator commented that his silent colleague is playing the role of a human lie detector, confirming truths and lies in his statements, and this aggravated his dilemma. Subsequently, while making disclosures, Jamal had demonstrated movements and changes in body language to hide from the attention of the silent interrogator. Based on such verbal and non-verbal responses, the interrogators could easily assess his deceptive and truthful disclosures. In effect, through this technique, Jamal himself had turned into a human lie detector.

To identify the truth and lies in the interrogatee's statements, Soufan suggests certain practical tips. No accused can stick to lies for long when questioned in minute detail. A key part of successful interrogations is to ask detailed questions related to time and whereabouts. Such questions are easy for an accused if he is telling the truth; but if he is lying, it is hard for him to keep the story straight. In the case of partial lies, interrogators can ascertain where he is lying by zeroing in on details. The process requires patience—interrogators can't show frustration. That would only encourage the accused to hold out, thinking the interrogator will soon give up. Instead, interrogators have to show that they are not in a rush and are prepared to spend as long as it takes. Persistence is of paramount importance. A mistake some interrogators make is giving an interrogation a fixed time slot. Doing so only alerts the accused to the fact that all he needs to do is outlast the interrogators during the scheduled time.

13

Interrogation of Women and Juveniles

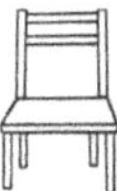

OF THE VARIOUS FACTORS that influence the outcome of any interrogation, the background characteristics of the suspect or accused are of crucial importance. Thus, how women and juvenile offenders approach an interrogation, and particularly the extent of their confession or admission of guilt is worth considering. Researchers and criminologists differ on this issue. For example, several British researchers[113] have found no gender differences in the rate of admissions and denials. Similarly, Leo[114] found no significant relationship between gender and likelihood of confession or self-incrimination. On the other hand, C Phillips and D Brown[115] found a significant gender difference, with females confessing more commonly than males. According to them, while the admission rate of females was 73%, that of the males was only 52%. In India, the confession rate among rural women offenders is high when compared to that of male offenders. However, there is some evidence that younger suspects are more likely to confess than older suspects. A 1970 US study[116] found that 42.9% of suspects under the age of 25 in Colorado confessed under police interrogation compared to 18.2% of older suspects. It has also been observed that juvenile suspects are more vulnerable and easily succumb to pressure and coercive tactics, leading to false confessions, as demonstrated in a number of sensational cases such as the Stefanie Crowe murder or the Central Park 5.

Thus, there has been increased recognition of the need to treat women and young offenders more sensitively than other offenders. The UN and its different agencies have adopted Conventions and guidelines for this. For example, the Convention on the Rights of the Child (CRC)[117] stipulates that "regardless of the situation, law enforcement officials are required to exercise particular care and sensitivity when dealing with children, thus preventing the law enforcement action from traumatizing them and causing them long-lasting harm." Article 40 of the CRC and the Beijing Rules,[118] while upholding the basic rights of any person deprived of freedom, stressed that parents and guardians should be involved when dealing with juvenile offenders, who should be detained separate from adults. Only female law enforcement personnel are empowered to arrest and conduct body searches of women. Similarly, female personnel should supervise the detention and interrogation of women offenders.

Nations have enacted a number of legislations to safeguard the rights and privileges of juvenile and women offenders during the different phases of the criminal justice process. In India, the Criminal Procedure Code (CrPC) lays down specific provisions to ensure special rights for children and women in relation to arrest or questioning. Some of these major provisions are:

Section 46(4) of CrPC: Police cannot arrest a woman between sunset and sunrise. Under exceptional circumstances, a lady police officer can arrest the woman concerned with written permission from the Magistrate.

The presence of a lady officer is mandatory when questioning a woman. It is also stipulated that their interrogation should be limited to a maximum of eight hours at a stretch and interrogations during the night need to be avoided.

In Sakshi v. Union of India,[119] the Apex Court discussed offenses such as rape against women and stressed the need to protect minor victims from all forms of sexual abuse in line with the articles and provisions of the CRC and the United Nations Convention on the Elimination of All Forms of Discrimination against Women. It also laid down guidelines on the investigation and trial of rape victims such as victims who are minors should be interrogated at their residence in the presence of relatives or family members.

Section 160(1) of CrPC: No male below the age of 15 or above the age of 65, or a woman, or a physically or mentally disabled person can be called to the police station for interrogation.

Juveniles need special attention: Apart from these legal provisions, interrogators should be extra cautious while interrogating juveniles. Some important guidelines are:

1. Interrogators should ascertain the age of the juvenile with the help of authentic documents or records. As per the Juvenile Justice (Care and Protection of Children) Act of 2015, any youth charged with a criminal law violation who is below the age of 18 at the time of the offense, arrest or

referral to court, may be treated as juvenile. Many times, the accused take the plea of being a juvenile in order to escape severe punishment. In the Nirbhaya case,[120] one of the accused tried to escape from the hangman's noose by claiming his juvenile status. His ploy failed, however, as investigators had established his actual age with the help of documents.

2. A juvenile's capacity to understand the legal and other procedures, as well as the questions posed needs to be ascertained before interrogation. Those who are mentally challenged or suffering from other ailments may not be in a position to understand the questions and procedures.

3. A juvenile is unable to waive constitutional rights such as the Miranda clause or the Right to Silence without consultation with an interested adult. This should be properly explained to the juvenile offender before initiating the interrogation The juvenile's parents or guardians should be kept abreast of such procedures.

There are four stages in the interrogation of a juvenile:

Rapport Building: The first stage is establishing better rapport with the juvenile, which on many instances can be tedious as the juvenile offender is in a state of trauma or anxiety in the presence of the interrogators. The interrogator should properly explain the aim of the questioning without creating fear or concern in the juvenile's mind. The special rights and privileges of the juvenile are to be explained. Through their interaction, the interrogator needs to assess the juvenile's social, cognitive and emotional development. The interrogator should ensure that the juvenile is in a position to understand the questions and distinguish between true and false statements.

Free narrative: In this stage, the role of the interrogator is to act as facilitator, starting with open-ended invitation questions (e.g., "What shall we talk about?"). The interrogators should try to free the juvenile from undue tension and anxiety. For that purpose, themes or subjects not related to the event or offense are discussed in a relaxed manner, followed by the juvenile's narration of the event. Interrogators should select the theme of interaction based on the biosocial profile of the subject or the areas of his or her interest. For example, a youth with an urban background may be more interested in an ongoing sports event, cricket match or recently released movie at the box office, whereas a rural youth may be more interested in his way of life, nature, habitat or the flora or fauna of his area.

Questioning: In this phase, the interrogator starts with open-ended specific questions—the 5 Ws + H (Who or Whom, What or Which, Where, When and Why + How). Examples are: "Where was Leena at that time?" "What did she do when you met her?" "Who was with her?") If needed, closed questions can be asked during the second stage (e.g., "Did she go downstairs? Yes or no?"). Interrogators should avoid repeating questions as far as possible during the free narrative stage as there are chances of the juvenile getting intimidated.

Closure: Interrogators should cross-check the details given by the subject. If necessary, questions can be repeated for clarity. The interrogator may give the suspect an opportunity to ask questions.

Sometimes, interrogators share their contact information with a suggestion that the juvenile can provide additional inputs if any. Normally the interrogation ends by discussing neutral topics or themes in order to reassure the juvenile.

Difficulties or problems: There are many impediments or difficulties in the interrogation of women and juveniles. First is the difficulty to establish rapport between the suspect and interrogators as many first-time offenders feel fear and anxiety, which create strong mental blocks. Interrogators need to adopt the right techniques to overcome their silent or passive mood. Any overbearing behaviour or questions from the interrogators would worsen the situation. Proper planning and preparation are essential in order to avoid such mistakes. Once rapport has been established, it is equally important to maintain the same throughout the interrogation. For that purpose, interrogators try to avoid repeat questions during the narration stage that will numb the suspect. The golden rule in the interrogation of juveniles is not to repeat questions that would be intimidating or would create fear in the mind of the juvenile. However, repeat questions are essential to check whether the juvenile understood the question or not. Secondly, meticulous planning is needed to structure the interrogation and frame proper questions. The 5 Ws + H questions are most effective in eliciting information. Frequent use of closed questions with younger children who didn't understand what was required is advisable.

14

Science and Technology in Interrogation

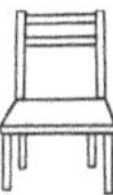

THE SEARCH FOR EFFECTIVE aids for interrogation is probably as old as man's need to obtain information from an uncooperative accused or suspect. In ancient times, many primitive practices or customs attributed to the divine had been ingeniously used to identify the real culprits. With the advancement of science and technology, criminologists and investigators have explored innovative technologies in different areas of investigation, including interrogation. The judiciary, too, has acknowledged the role of science and technology in the criminal justice system. As rightly stated by Justice Stephen Breyer of the US Supreme Court, "in the age of science, science should expect to find warm welcome, perhaps a permanent home, in our courtrooms... our decisions should reflect proper scientific and technical understanding so that the law can respond to the needs of the public."[121]

The twenty-first century has witnessed an explosion in the types and quality of technology available for intelligence and security organizations. However, there was not a corresponding advancement in identifying, developing and fielding technologies in the field of interrogation. Advancements in the field of psychophysiology, a branch of science that studies subtle physiological changes such as respiration, heartbeat, skin surface temperature paved the way for the introduction of specific technologies in criminal investigations. The basic concept was that these technologies can measure autonomic and somatic responses in order to detect deception by a suspect during interrogation. The lie detector or the Polygraph test, the P300 or the Brain Mapping test and the narcoanalysis or the Truth Serum test are the three main tests that have been used during interrogation to extract confessions or to interpret the behaviour of a criminal or a suspect. Other techniques include the Electrogastrogram, radar vital signs monitor, voice stress analysis and thermal imaging.

The polygraph is the most widely employed technical means for detecting deception. The operation of the polygraph is based on the assumption that certain physiological responses occur when a person is confronted with an offense or crime under investigation and that this reaction would have detectable external manifestations. There is a long history of the transformation of the polygraph as a mechanism for detecting lies. In 1730, the British novelist Daniel Defoe, in an article on the schemes to prevent street robberies and other crimes during the night, advanced a theory that the pulse of a suspect can reveal whether he is lying or not. More than a century later, the Italian physiologist Angelo Mosso developed an instrument called plethysmograph to detect changes in blood pressure in response to certain stimuli. In

1892, Sir James Mackensie constructed the first instrument for the polygraph test. However, it was Cesare Lombroso, an Italian criminologist and psychiatrist in 1895 who used it as a scientific instrument to measure physiological changes in the blood pressure and pulse of a suspect under interrogation. In 1921, John Augustus Larson, a Canadian psychologist employed in the Berkeley Police Department in California, invented the primitive form of this instrument and named it Polygraph. Larson was the first person to use this instrument to continuously and simultaneously measure the heart rate, blood pressure and respiratory variations of a person during interrogation. Leonarde Keeler of California, USA, in 1939, patented what is considered to be prototype of the modern polygraph—the Keeler Polygraph.

The polygraph underwent further innovations in the computer age when John Hopkins Laboratory in Maryland, USA developed a software named Poly-Score—a sophisticated mathematical algorithm to analyze polygraph data in order to assess the probability of lies or truthfulness of a suspect. The psycho-galvanometer is one of the latest devices that is used to record the skin's electrical resistance. In the wake of controversies on the effectiveness of the polygraph in crime detection, in 2003, the National Academy of Sciences, US reviewed the scientific evidence on the value of the polygraph and concluded that although there may be alternate techniques to polygraph testing, none can outperform the polygraph and none seemed promising enough to supplant the polygraph in the near future. Thus, over 70 years after the introduction of the polygraph, Dr Kristin Heckman and Mark Happel contend that "despite the polygraph's shortcomings, there is currently no viable technical alternative to polygraphy."[122]

In a polygraph test, the signs of the interaction between mind and body of a suspect subjected to the interrogation are monitored by the sensors of a polygraph machine attached to his or her body. When the suspect lies, it is accompanied by specific, perceptible physiological and behavioural changes such as high blood pressure, pulse rate, respiration, skin resistance and muscle movements. These changes are amplified and recorded onto a multichannel writing device. The investigators analyze the pattern in the chart along with clinical experts and arrive at conclusions.

The polygraph test is conducted in three phases: a pre-test interview, chart recording, and diagnosis. The pre-test interview, according to Douglas Wicklander,[123] an expert in new interrogation mechanisms, is an effective means to identify the suspect's true status, independent of the polygraph. He found that the suspect's physical and verbal responses prior to the test helped investigators have a better understanding of the baseline behaviour of the suspect. The polygraph pre-test gives the examiner a check and balance against later polygraph charts to assist in a correct truth or deception conclusion.

As a part of chart recording, the polygraph is used in conjunction with one or more related tests such as the Guilty Knowledge Test (GKT) or Concealed Information Test; the Comparison Question Test or Control Question Test (CQT); or the Relevant/Irrelevant Test (RIT). These tests are based on a set of questions that include the criminal charges against the accused and statements made by him or her at various stages of the investigation. They are meant to ascertain the subject's baseline response and for comparing the responses to assess the extent of truthfulness in his or her replies. Normally, a sensible person's replies to irrelevant questions would be negative. (For e.g., an irrelevant question such as "Are you wearing a gown?" when the lady undergoing the test is in a sari.) Though Relevant and Control questions are related to the offense, they are used to compare the responses. For instance, "Have you stolen $500 from Robert's cupboard?" is a relevant question in the investigation of a theft case, while "Have you ever stolen money from your employer?" is a control question generally connected with the offense of theft. The accused alone will know the answer to Concealed questions, for example, "Where did you conceal the weapon used to strike the lady?" An innocent person is unable to answer such a concealed question.

Narcoanalysis or the Truth Serum test: The research by Robert House, a Dallas, Texas physician, on the impact of certain drugs like scopolamine on the central nervous system had led to the use of Narcoanalysis for criminal investigations. He found that scopolamine, along with morphine and chloroform, could induce a state of "twilight sleep" during childbirth. In 1922, it occurred to Robert House that a similar technique could be employed in the interrogation of suspected criminals and he successfully demonstrated the test on two prisoners in the Dallas county jail. Thus, Robert House concluded that a person under the influence of scopolamine "cannot create a lie... and there is no power to think or reason."

Subsequent research by criminologists and medical professionals has established that certain drugs like scopolamine, sodium amytal and sodium pentothal can produce sedation and drowsiness, confusion and disorientation, incoordination and amnesia in a person. Because of such properties, sodium amytal and sodium pentothal are used most commonly as anaesthetics. Some of these drugs, best described as truth serums, have been administered to suspects during interrogation. The assumption is that suspects under the influence of the serum will respond to the interrogator's questions with truthful statements or answers that he believed to be truthful. In reality, truth serums do not force a suspect to tell the truth, instead they put the suspect in a hypnotic stance and cause him or her to become more open and talkative, shedding all inhibitions.

To conduct the test, 3g of sodium pentothal or sodium amytal is dissolved in 3000 ml of distilled water. Depending on the suspect's sex, age, health and physical condition, this solution is administered intravenously along with 10% of dextrose for three hours with the help of an anaesthetist. The effect of the bio-molecules on the bio-activity of an individual is evident as the drug depresses the central nervous system, lowers blood pressure and slows the heart rate, putting the suspect into a hypnotic trance resulting in a lack of inhibition. The suspect is then interrogated in the presence of a clinical expert or medical professional. Revelations made during this stage are recorded both in video and audio cassettes. The experts prepare the report, which is then used in the process of collecting evidence. Personal consent of the suspect is ensured before undertaking the test.

Brain Fingerprinting, P300-MERMER: Pioneering research in this field dates back to the late 1980s when researchers like Rosenfeld (1987) and Donchin and Farwell (1991) successfully used Electroencephalography (EEG) to identify specific Event Related Potentials (ERPs) that were correlated to the recognition of guilty knowledge. But it was Dr Lawrence A Farwell, chairman of the Brain Wave Institute, Fairfield, USA who developed and patented the brain fingerprinting technique in 1995. This technique is based on the theory that the human brain plans, records and executes all the actions. In interrogation, this technique is used to ascertain whether the suspect can recognize specific inputs related to a crime or incident by measuring electrical brain wave responses or stimuli to words or images flashed across a computer screen. For that purpose, interrogators should have a sufficient amount of specific information about the crime or the incident, information that would only be known to the perpetrator. That is why brain fingerprinting is described by many as a type of Guilty Knowledge Test.

The entire operation is computer-controlled, including presentation of the stimuli and recording electrical brain activity, as well as a mathematical data analysis of responses. Sensors on a headband produce the suspect's EEG or brain signal reaction to the images. The EEG is fed into a processor that uses proprietary software to display and interpret the effects on the brain. A specific electrical brain sign reaction, known as P300, is emitted only when the suspect recognizes audios or images connected with the crime or incident. When the suspect sees an irrelevant image or input the brain does not consider it important or notable and a P300 is not emitted. Further research on P300 responses led to a larger theory named Memory and Encoding Related Multifaceted Electroencephalographic Response (MERMER), an advanced technique to interpret stimuli and responses through Many-sided Electroencephalographic Reaction Study (MERS).

A related technique is **Magnetoencephalography (MEG)**, in which a weak magnetic field produced due to the flow of electrical currents during neuronal activation is measured with the help of a magnetometer placed outside the suspect's skull. The area of the brain that has been activated by a stimulus can be localized by detecting the magnetic fields measured by a series of MEG recordings. In this technique, previously viewed stimuli and new stimuli flash across a computer screen in front of the suspects. They are instructed to respond based on the type of memory they have for the stimulus. If they can recollect the exact episode in which they saw the stimulus, they give a "remember" response; if they have a "feeling of knowing" the stimulus, they give a "know" response. Finally, if the suspects believe that they have never seen the stimulus before, they give a "new" response. Based on the analysis of these responses, experts can arrive at conclusions about their involvement or otherwise in the particular offense or incident.

Based on the various physiological and neurological changes that are detectable in a suspect subjected to interrogation, a number of other scientific mechanisms have been developed to aid interrogation. Some of the major techniques include:

Electrogastrogram (EGG): The EGG is a device used to diagnose the improper functioning of stomach muscles or of the nerves controlling those muscles. In normal condition, the stomach pulses three times per minute. Researchers (Hutson, 2005) have established that the gastrointestinal tract, which is uniquely sensitive to mental stress, shows variations in pulse rate. This is due to the communication between the central nervous system and the enteric nervous system. Electrodes placed on the stomach surface of a suspect measure the electrical waves, or pulses, as they progress downward from the top of the stomach. This enables interrogators to draw conclusions on the attitude of the suspect towards interrogation.

Thermal Imaging: This method is used to assess the veracity or otherwise of a suspect's revelations by scientifically analyzing the physiological changes, particularly those of the skin. Skin surface temperature (SST) is influenced by a number of factors such as blood circulation and the changes in the epithelial cells beneath the skin. Additional factors like stress, fear, embarrassment and sweating also effect changes in facial SST. A technique known as thermography measures the radiant energy or natural heat (infrared) emissions from the human body. Infrared radiometry is another advanced technology to measure body surface heat via camera, without skin contact. The camera is connected to and controlled by a personal computer running software designed for thermal imaging. The main advantage of this technique for interrogation is that it can be conducted non-invasively, covertly and in real time.

Radar Vital Signs Monitor (RVSM): This technology was developed at the Georgia Tech Research Institute, USA through a series of research projects part of clinical studies on breath rate, heartbeat, etc. In interrogation, this technique is used to analyze psychophysiological motion processes such as a suspect's heartbeat, respiration and eye blinks using electromagnetic waves in the gigahertz frequency range.

Advancements in the field of neuroscience and revolutionary improvements in neuroscientific techniques have enabled interrogators to systematically analyze various neurophysiological processes of the brain and how they impact the responses and behaviour of a suspect during interrogation. **Positron Emission Tomography (PET)**, a medical imaging technique developed in the early 1970s that uses nuclear medicine was a major step in this direction. The device is a PET scanner, which produces 3-dimensional images of a functional brain. During the imaging process, a radio-labelled positron emitting tracer is injected into a suspect's bloodstream. This tracer moves through the blood to different parts of the body, including the brain. The rate of blood flow to the brain depends on the level and location of neural activity. Factors such as fear, anger, anxiety influence neural activity. Areas of higher blood flow will contain a larger amount of the radioactive tracer, and will therefore emit stronger signals. Interrogators instruct the suspect to view images related to experienced and unexperienced events and to give their answers (lies). During both types of deception, the dorsolateral, ventrolateral and medial prefrontal cortices were active. The anterior cingulate cortex was active only during the kind of deception in which subjects were pretending not to know. The PET scanner measures the signals and scans slices of the brain which are then analyzed to reach conclusions on the veracity of the suspect's statements.

Functional Magnetic Resonance Imaging (fMRI) is a neuro-imaging technique that was developed in the early 1990s and has since become the preferred tool in the interrogation of terrorists and extremists in many countries such as the US. In this technique, the suspect's head is placed in a donut-shaped magnetic device which can detect subtle changes in electromagnetic fields. During interrogation, when the suspect uses any part of the brain for any activity, blood flow is directed to that region(s). Haemoglobin—an oxygen carrying protein in blood cells—exhibits different magnetic properties between oxygenated and de-oxygenated blood. Thus, by using fMRI and by analyzing the different emitted signals, interrogators can gain a better understanding of the brain areas that are active when the suspect was experiencing emotions such as anger, fear, anxiety, happiness or stress. Based on the fMRI spatial images, interrogators, to a great extent, can distinguish between deceptive and truthful responses of the suspect.

Computer Voice Stress Analysis (CVSA): Interrogators use this technique to assess the extent of truth or deception in a suspect's disclosures by analyzing variation in the sound module of the suspect during interrogation. A particular device developed by Charles R McQuiston in 1964 has been used in this technique. This machine detects laryngeal micro-tremors in the voice. When a person is under considerable stress, blood flow to the vocal cords diminishes, and as a result, the micro-tremors disappear or get blocked. The voice stress analyzer searches for the disappearance of this normal tremor when the suspects speak. US law enforcement and investigation agencies widely used this technique during the interrogation of suspects in a number of sensational cases such as the Stephanie Crowe murder case. However, its reliability and accuracy has come under scrutiny. Thus, in 2002, the US Department of Justice concluded that it is unlikely that a single measure such as that based on the CVSA, could be universally successful in assessing stress. It was also established that under extreme levels of stress, the contraction and relaxation of muscles throughout the body, including the muscles associated with speech production, will be affected. As the level and degree of this muscle control process determines the extent and nature of fluctuations in the speech signal, the latter cannot be conclusively determined. Moreover, even if these tremors exist, their influence will mostly be suspect-dependent. Of late, Artificial Intelligence (AI)-oriented technologies are being explored to overcome such loopholes in techniques like CVSA.

Advancements in cyberspace and innovations on the electronic front have been extensively used in different tools of criminal investigations, including interrogation. The audio monitoring of accused persons in detention enables investigators to collect vital clues related to the crime or incident, which can be effectively used for their interrogation. During World War II, both the US Strategic Interrogation Programme and the British MI-5 Interrogation Group relied heavily on the monitoring or recording of conversations among the prisoners. Such operations revealed that even senior German officers and trained intelligence operatives routinely disclosed sensitive information that they had tactfully withheld from the interrogators in conversation with their cellmates. In the twenty-first century, cybernetics and electronics have opened up spectacular opportunities that could facilitate an unprecedented level of surreptitious audio and video monitoring of detainees on a 24/7 basis.

Enforcement agencies have underscored the importance of recording interrogations, especially in sensitive cases. Videotaping interrogation has been legally enforced in the US, UK, Australia and other countries. Surreptitious videotaping has many advantages. Foremost, it relieves the interrogators from taking notes during the interrogation, thereby enabling them to closely observe and analyze the suspect's psychophysical cues relating to deception. The simple act of taking notes, on many occasions, creates apprehensions in the suspect's mind that all his disclosures are being recorded and could be used as evidence against him. This could create mental blocks and deter the suspect from speaking the truth. Secondly, interrogators can use recordings as a protective shield against allegations of mistreatment of the accused or prisoner abuse. Finally, recordings can be used as a teaching tool for interrogation techniques.

There has been much debate about the reliability and legality of scientific aids and techniques and the ethical implications of their use. The US Supreme Court succinctly put it as, "there are important differences between the quest for truth in the courtroom and the quest for truth in the laboratory. Scientific conclusions are subject to perpetual revision. Law, on the other hand, must resolve disputes finally and quickly."[124] As many of these techniques are incipient constantly under revision or updation, they can neither be fully relied upon during criminal investigation nor can the evidence adduced through their application be treated as conclusive. For example, in the case of narcoanalysis, the Supreme Court of New Jersey concluded in 1989 that the results of a sodium amytal interview (narco test) are not considered scientifically reliable for the purpose of ascertaining the truth.[125] Nevertheless, many courts in the US and elsewhere endorsed the results of sodium amytal as useful in criminal investigations and during the trial of the cases.

The situation is not different in India. Narcoanalysis and other techniques like P300 brain mapping have raised scientific, constitutional, legal and ethical issues. However, these tests have been used in the investigation of a good number of cases, including some high-profile ones. More importantly, some of the High Courts also accorded permission to conduct such tests on accused persons with the findings that these tests did not violate the provisions of Article 20(3) of the Constitution of India, which ensure the Right against Self-incrimination. For example, in Dinesh Dalmia v. State,[126] the Madras High Court examined the issue and held that subjecting an accused to narcoanalysis did not tantamount to testimony by compulsion and "revelations during such tests is quite voluntary." Thus, the accused cannot claim the protective provision under Article 20(3). Similarly, in 2004, the Bombay High Court in the fake stamp paper case maintained that subjecting an accused to certain tests like narcoanalysis did not violate the fundamental Right against Self-incrimination. In Ramchandra Ram Reddy and Others v. The State of Maharashtra,[127] the Bombay High Court upheld the legality of the use of polygraph, brain mapping (P300) and narcoanalysis during investigations.

Similarly, in a number of cases, the Supreme Court of India has granted permission to investigation agencies to conduct such tests on the accused persons, under specific conditions. On the question of forcible application of the narcoanalysis test on the accused, as raised in RB Sharma v. State of Maharashtra, the Apex Court had quoted from a case from the US in Frye v. United States as, "Just when a scientific principle of discovery crosses the line between the experimental stand and demonstrable state is difficult to define. Somewhere in the twilight zone, the evidential force must be recognized and while the court will go a long way in admitting the expert testimony deducted from a well-recognized scientific principle or discovery, the thing from which the deduction is made must be sufficiently established to have gained general acceptance in the particular field to which it belongs."[128] Quoting from another US case (Daubert v. Merrell Dow Pharmaceuticals[129]), the SC clarified that the courts may consider factors such as reliability, peer review to publication potential for error and general acceptance by community for the admissibility of scientific evidence.

The Apex Court has put at rest all disputes about the constitutionality or legality of application of all such tests by its verdict in the case of Selvi and Others v. State of Karnataka.[130] This 2004 case related to the murder of Kavita and her husband Shivakumar, who got married against the wishes of Kavita's family. Selvi, Kavita's mother, and two other persons were named as the main suspects in the case. Since the prosecution based its case entirely on circumstantial evidence, it sought the court's permission to conduct polygraph and brain mapping tests on the suspects, which the court granted. As the polygraph tests showed deception, the prosecution sought permission to conduct narcoanalysis tests. The suspects who were unwilling to go under narco tests challenged the order of the Magistrate before the High Court of Karnataka, which rejected the plea. On an appeal by the accused, the SC made it clear that nobody can be compelled to undergo narcoanalysis, brain mapping or lie detector tests and any statements made during these procedures are not admissible as evidence. Such tests are permissible only when they are taken voluntarily. The Court found that narcoanalysis and brain mapping tests violate the provisions under Article 20(3) of the Constitution of India.

Despite such legal restrictions, the application of scientific tools in the administration criminal justice system is gaining more and more acceptance. Justice VJ Malimath, who headed the Committee on Reforms of the criminal justice system (2003), had succinctly put it as, "it can hardly be overemphasized that interview of witnesses or interrogation of suspects or accused should be done in a professional manner to elicit truth. This is possible only when the Investigation officer has professional competence, adequate time at his disposal and the interview or interrogation is conducted in a proper ambience."[131] The biggest challenge for the agencies is how these tools can be effectively used to generate inputs that can avert terror strikes or other organized crimes while upholding the due process of law. Another area of concern is the false confessions by the suspects, which lead to a miscarriage of justice. Taking such factors into account, many countries have formulated new interrogation standards which include: minimizing the use of psychologically manipulative techniques; video recording of custodial interrogations; better training for improving professionalism of interrogators and special precautionary measures in the interrogation of vulnerable suspects, such as juveniles and women. Naturally, such measures will make the evidence generated through interrogation more reliable.

15

Looking Ahead

How can Interrogation Be Improved?

"YOU SHALL KNOW THE truth, and the truth will make you free" (John 8: 31-32). This Biblical injunction is the real purpose of interrogation—to elicit the truth from the suspect or accused. The crucial question is, how potent is this weapon to elicit the truth? In the words of Dr Robert Coulam, "there is little systematic knowledge available to tell us 'what works' in interrogation. We do not know what methods or processes of interrogation best protect the nation's security."[132] Such questions have become more relevant in the twenty-first century when law enforcement and security or intelligence agencies widely use the tool of interrogation for a myriad of tasks such as investigations, collection of intelligence or national security related inputs. It is a well-established fact that police interrogation accounts for almost 90% of all investigation work. And it is the same with other enforcement agencies that, in one way or another, use interrogation for various operational purposes.

Thus, it is relevant to examine how the tool of interrogation can be sharpened and polished in order to meet new challenges. The first task is to ensure its credibility and reliability so that the evidence or inputs generated through this process should find due place in the criminal justice process or in the internal security architecture. This has become all the more significant in the light of the large number of false confessions and distorted inputs elicited during interrogations. A false confession is not only useless but also completely derails the investigation, as the real perpetrator roams free whereas the innocent are implicated in the crime. Similarly, half-baked or unreliable intelligence is of little use in countering serious national security threats. And when such episodes come to light, public confidence in law enforcement and security agencies take a nosedive, which, according to Gudjonsson, demoralizes the agencies and leads to corruption and other malpractices. The best examples are the Stephanie Crowe murder case[133] in California and the Central Park 5 case[134] in New York City, which created so much public criticism against the police or investigators for their lack of professionalism and competence. In India, the 2008 Aarushi murder case opened up a Pandora's box of critical issues of criminal investigations, including false confessions and misuse of narcoanalysis tests.

False confessions, as we have discussed earlier, occur due to a confluence of factors such as the personal (psychological) vulnerabilities of suspects and the use of accusatorial or coercive interrogative methods. The incidence of such confessions increases when overzealous interrogators with tunnel vision operate as human lie detectors and identify suspects based on certain preconceived assumptions and vigorously pursue their sole agenda of extracting a confession. False confessions obtained through coercive and manipulative interrogation techniques get exposed during the trial stage, causing much embarrassment or a boomerang effect to the investigators or interrogators. They also adversely reflect on the functioning of law enforcement and security agencies.

The main result of the boomerang effect is reforms or changes in the criminal justice system, including investigations and interrogations. For example, the exposure of false confessions in a number of sensational cases in the UK led to serious research into various interrogation models or techniques (Bull and Soukara, 2010).[135] Such endeavours resulted in the development of information-gathering methods of interrogation with minimum use of psychologically manipulative techniques, proper recording of custodial interrogation, enhanced training of interrogators and special precautions during the interrogation of vulnerable suspects. Of utmost importance was that interrogators were prohibited from using deceptive mechanisms to extract false confessions from suspects. Other countries such as Norway, New Zealand and Australia have amended their interrogation practices, focusing more on information-gathering processes. Similarly, influenced by the United Nations Declaration of Human Rights and campaigns of other human rights bodies such as European Convention of Human Rights (ECHR), many European countries have introduced new techniques of interrogation, including the ban on closed-ended or confirmatory questions and deception in the interrogation of suspects.

Similar research[136] was undertaken on the merits and demerits of accusatorial and information-gathering methods of interrogation, especially after the extensive use of coercive techniques by the US in their fight against global terrorism. The declared policy of the US that such methods were most successful in containing the threat of terror or extremist outfits has created controversy within the US and the comity of nations around the world. For example, the 2014 Senate Report of the Senate Select Committee on Intelligence,[137] on the CIA's enhanced interrogation strategies, felt that these techniques were based more on intimidation, coercion or aggression and had conflicted directly with the existing practices that highlighted the value of rapport building and interpersonal skill on the part of the interrogators. Their observations were almost in line with the findings of researchers like Meissner, Hartwig and Russano (2010)[138] that accusatorial methods increase the likelihood of false confessions, while information-gathering methods protect the innocent yet preserve the interrogator's ability to elicit confessions from guilty persons. These factors have influenced countries like Canada, which have been slowly switching over to the information-gathering model. The heart of the matter is that no single interrogation method or technique can be prescribed for every suspect or interrogatee. These methods differ for suspects of different ages, cultures, ethnicities, criminal background or for crimes of greater seriousness such as terrorism and extremism.

As interrogation is basically an art, the performers (interrogators) decide the success or failure of the performance. How can they excel in this art? There needs to be enough and dedicated manpower and policy on recruitment, training and deployment. Conceptually, almost all agencies agree that only highly skilled, educated, motivated and specialized personnel be recruited or chosen as interrogators. But the reality is that, for the most part, interrogations are conducted by law enforcement personnel with widely divergent skills, education and experience. In many countries, including the US, interrogation is not considered a speciality but one of the many skills required by an investigator or law enforcement personnel. Very often, ad-hoc arrangements have been made to meet exigencies. For example, after 9/11, the US military and other government entities engaged novice interrogators, after just a six-week training course and without having ever conducted a real interrogation, let alone interrogating al-Qaeda terrorists. When such inexperienced interrogators started their own interrogations, they didn't have much success and began trying different methods to get information. This led to a series of disagreements between experienced and novice interrogators on the manner of conducting interrogation of dreaded al-Qaeda operatives such as Nasser al-Bahri and Mohammed al-Qahtani.[139] The situation is worse in many countries where herds of personnel are deployed for the interrogation of dreaded terrorists or insurgents, despite lacking knowledge of basic interrogation techniques.

The second factor is training. Almost all law enforcement or intelligence agencies impart basic training on interrogation to their personnel. But in the majority of instances, this training comes under the domain of criminal investigations, sometimes with some focus on counter-insurgency or counter-terrorist operations. Accordingly, interrogation is just one among the many modules in the training of newly inducted personnel in these agencies, followed by periodic in-service courses. This is inadequate to impart required skills and expertise to the personnel for interrogation. In the words of the former FBI agent Ali Soufan, "interrogation skills and knowledge cannot be picked up from a few training sessions; they come from studying the groups and the subject, and lots of interrogation experience working alongside experts."[140] Captain Albert F Pierce of the Massachusetts Institute of Technology (MIT) Police Department, who had long innings in the Massachusetts state police as interrogator has succinctly put it as, "if a young detective is lucky enough to be partnered with an experienced, successful mentor, that mentor will be the most useful source of interrogation training. As a corollary, one must assume that if the partner is not helpful or is inexperienced, young detectives will have to learn the techniques on their own."[141]

To learn the art on their own, a few factors are essential. The first one is continuity in the job. As the popular dictum goes that "a rolling stone gathers no moss," so, too, personnel deployed for a wide range of tasks can neither concentrate in the area of interrogation nor get an opportunity to develop their skills and expertise to emerge as successful interrogators. Many agencies have formed separate units or wings for the exclusive task of interrogation. The personnel of such units may be provided enough incentives or motivation to make positive efforts to develop their skills. Basically, there are three major barriers of success in interrogation: linguistic or cultural barriers, scientific or technical or subject matter barriers, and interpersonal or intrapersonal barriers. An interrogation set-up with a multicultural-linguistic complexion and personnel with better knowledge, skills and understanding on new areas of science and technology and who excel in inter- and intrapersonal relations and behaviour, can definitely overcome such barriers. For example, interrogators who can easily identify the unique cultural traits and habits of the suspects are better placed to establish rapport with them. Similarly, the advantages of multilingual interrogators are undeniable. Moreover, interpersonal relations or behaviour assume considerable importance. Truly liking people, an ability to get along with people of all backgrounds, comfort in talking to people and knowledge of how to do it are essential to develop such special skills. In this regard, Pierce narrated in an interview that he as a young interrogator, developed such skills by sitting outside or in bars with his partner and observing and speaking with people so that he could learn these skills and improve on whatever innate abilities he already possessed.[142] In many instances, seasoned interrogators attend courtroom proceedings in order to get a first-hand account of potential problems with interrogation procedures, especially the questions and tactics used by defence attorneys to demolish the evidence collected through interrogation.

Law enforcement and investigative agencies need to provide adequate resources to their personnel to develop skills and expertise. Videos containing the latest techniques and technologies used in different methods of interrogation should be made available to the training establishments. Even Robotics and Artificial Intelligence (AI) have been used to properly assess body language, facial expressions and tonality of suspects during interrogation. The new generation of interrogators should be kept abreast of such innovations. Similarly, an interrogator's knowledge and understanding of various techniques of interrogation needs to be updated with the help of videos displaying successful interrogations of different categories of suspects, including terrorists or extremists and espionage agents. This has become all the more important in view of the rapid spread of newer and hitherto unknown types of crimes and the ingenious mechanisms adopted by the perpetrators with impunity. In order to keep abreast of such trends, there needs to be continuous awareness research on all such themes. The various training establishments of the police and other intelligence or investigation agencies can set up study centres either independently or in collaboration with renowned research bodies and universities to keep on updating all relevant knowledge and information of all such progressions. Such a database at the central and state levels will be of immense help to interrogators in both law enforcement interrogations and intelligence interrogations.

Another area that needs serious attention is the changes or amendments in existing laws and procedures that govern criminal investigations, particularly interrogation. Such amendments have become crucial in view of the transition in the nature and dimensions of crimes and the emergence of organized crimes such as terrorism and extremism. Concepts like the Miranda clause or the Right to Silence and other legal and constitutional safeguards for an accused or suspect have to be seen in this context, especially in light of the evolving international opinion that global peace and stability need to be maintained even by using extreme measures. Many countries like the US and Israel have adopted extreme steps in their fight against global terrorism.

India has been a victim of terrorism and depredations of non-state actors and has been contemplating such changes for a long time. A number of government committees such as Dr Justice VS Malimath Committee on Reforms of the Criminal Justice System (2003),[143] Dr NR Madhav Menon Committee on a Draft National Policy on Criminal Justice (2007), and the Second Administrative Reforms Commission headed by Dr Veerappa Moily (2005), and independent think tanks have studied these issues in detail and made a number of recommendations for specific changes to the Code of Criminal Procedure, 1973, and the Indian Evidence Act, 1872, so that many legal and procedural constraints that hinder the effective functioning of law enforcement agencies can be overcome. One specific proposal pertained to major changes in the Indian Evidence Act, particularly in sections 24 to 27, so that a confession made by an accused before a police officer would be admissible evidence. Citing the sunset principle,[144] legal luminaries like Justice (retired) VR Krishna Iyer of the Supreme Court favoured such changes. The Law Commission of India, in its 69th report has also made similar suggestions.[145]

Though this proposal had seized the attention of the Executive and the Legislature, no positive decision has been taken as it is linked to the professionalism and functioning of law enforcement agencies, particularly the police. The architects of the Indian Evidence Act had clearly reflected on this approach, as seen from the comments of the report of the Select Committee on the Draft Bill of the Evidence Act, 1871: "We have not thought it necessary to transfer from the present position in CrPC rules to the confession made to the police. This appears to be a special matter relating rather to the discipline of police than to the principles of evidence.[146] The million-dollar question is whether our enforcement or investigation agencies could improve their image as truly professional outfits deeply committed to the canons of law and due process, and be free from extraneous forces or influences. If they emerge as true professional organizations fully committed to the rule of law, such amendments are welcome.

It is equally important to ensure a conducive working environment for interrogators by providing adequate logistics and resources. In this regard, the Malimath Committee made some worthwhile suggestions which include: a) better application of scientific aids and technology to enhance the professional competence of interrogators and to create proper ambience during interrogation, b) establishment of well-planned interrogation centres in all district headquarters with better facilities and amenities so that interrogators can undertake interrogations in a legal and humane way and c) video recording of all interrogations and use of data for strengthening prosecution evidence and blunting the allegations of excesses during interrogation. Though some new initiatives have been taken in this direction in a few states under the Modernization of Police Programme (MPP), overall, the progress in improving interrogation infrastructure and logistics continue to remain tardy.

After all, law enforcement or investigation agencies seldom perceive interrogation as a speciality, rather, they treat it as one of the many skills required by an investigator or law enforcement personnel. There is also the misconception that any personnel can undertake this exercise and produce results. As revealed by Ali Soufan, even agencies like the CIA engage novices in this field to interrogate hardcore terrorists and pressurize them to produce results. Such flexible options coupled with ad-hoc arrangements during exigencies hinder the proper training or in-service courses for personnel exclusively meant for interrogation. In most police organizations, over 80% of the personnel do not receive any basic training or in-service training in interrogation. The situation is not different in the case of investigative or other agencies. In many instances, such raw hands, devoid of a basic understanding of the art of interrogation are deployed for sensitive interrogation tasks. So long such an approach continues in law enforcement investigation and security agencies, the real aim of interrogation will remain an unfulfilled dream.

Notes

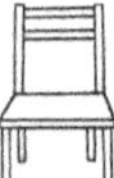

1. The Old Testament (Genesis 4:8-11).
2. The Old Testament (The Book of Kings I 3:16-28).
3. T Eric Peet, "The Great Tomb Robberies of the Ramesside Age. Papyri Mayer A and B," *The Journal of* 2, no. 1 (1915): 204-206.
4. *Chanakya Niti* is a collection of aphorisms composed by Chanakya. It is a set of ideas and statements, many of which give valuable tips on how to govern a state.
5. The Spanish Inquisition was a judicial institution that lasted from 1478 to 1834. Its ostensible purpose was to combat heresy in Spain, but, in practice, it consolidated power in the monarchy of the newly unified Spanish kingdom. Its brutal methods led to widespread death and suffering.
6. In American history, the Salem witch trials, June 1692 to May 1693, were a series of investigations and persecutions that caused 19 convicted "witches" to be hanged and many other suspects to be imprisoned in Salem Village in the Massachusetts Bay Colony.

7. Paul Cohen, "Torture and Translation in the Multilingual Courtrooms of Early Modern France," *Renaissance Quarterly* 69, no. 3 (2016): 899-939.

8. Edward Peters, Torture: Expanded Edition (Philadelphia, University of Pennsylvania Press, 1966).

9. Aleksandr Solzhenitsyn, "Interrogation," excerpt from *The Gulag Archipelago*, Harper's Magazine, 1974, last accessed January 12, 2024, https://harpers.org/archive/2014/07/interrogation.

10. The National Commission on Law Observance and Enforcement was a committee established by US president Herbert Hoover in 1929, and submitted this report in 1931.

11. Brown v. Mississippi, 297 U.S. 278 (1936).

12. The Phoenix Program was designed and initially coordinated by the CIA during the Vietnam war to contain the Vietnam underground forces (Viet-Cong).

13. Operation Condor was a formal system to coordinate repression among the countries of the Southern Cone that operated from the mid-1970s until the early 1980s. It aimed to persecute and eliminate political, social, trade-union and student activists from Argentina, Uruguay, Chile, Paraguay, Bolivia and Brazil.

14. Convened in 1949 on the earlier treaties for the protection of war victims—revising and updating them into 4 new conventions comprising 429 articles of law, known as the Geneva Conventions of August 12, 1949.

15. Hanns Scharff was a German Luftwaffe interrogator during the Second World War. He has been called the "Master Interrogator" of the Luftwaffe and possibly of all Nazi Germany. He has also been praised for his contribution to US interrogation techniques after the war.

16 Sherwood Ford Moran (1885–1983) was a US Marine Major who, after serving as a congregational missionary in Japan, fought in the Second World War as an interrogator of POWs and soon after became known for his memorandum on the efficacy of humane forms of interrogation.

17. The Vienna Declaration and Programme of Action was the main outcome of the World Conference on Human Rights held in Vienna, Austria from June 14 to June 25, 1993. The Declaration marked "the culmination of a long process of review and debate over the current status of human rights machinery in the world and accepted the universality of human rights."

18. Criminal terms glossary by Federal Bureau of Investigation (FBI).

19. *Educing Information: Interrogation: Science and Art*, 2006. Google Books.

20. Steven Kleinman, "*The History of MIS-Y: U.S. Strategic Interrogation During World War II*" (master's thesis, Joint Military Intelligence College, 2002).

21. Fadia M Narchet, Christian A Meissner and Melissa B Russano, "Modelling the Influence of Investigator Bias on the Elicitation of True and False Confessions,» *Law and Human Behavior* 35, no. 6 (2011): 452-465.

22. Richard Leo, "Inside the Interrogation Room," *Journal of Criminal Law and Criminology* 86, no. 2 (1996): 266-303.

23. Lawrence S Leiken, "Police Interrogation in Colorado: The Implementation of Miranda," *Denver Law Journal* 47, no. 1 (1970).

24. See Moston note 195; also see J Pearse et al., "Police Interviewing and Psychological Vulnerabilities: Predicting the Likelihood of a Confession," *Journal of Community and Applied Social Psychology* 8, no. 1 (1998); see also Richard Leo.

25. Coretta Phillips and David Brown, "Entry into the Criminal Justice System: A Survey of Police Arrests and their Outcomes," Home Office Research Study no. 185 (1998).

26. Samkhya is one of India's six philosophical schools (darshans). Samkhya maintains a coherent dualism between matter (Prakriti) and the eternal spirit (Purusha). Purusha and Prakriti are initially distinct but, over time, Purusha mistakenly connects itself with parts of Prakriti.

27. Vasishtha is known as the priest and preceptor, teacher of the Ikshvaku king's clan. He was also the preceptor of Manu, the progenitor of Kshatriyas and Sakthi.

28. Jitatmananda S, "Consciousness: Evolution of Life through Higher Mind," Life, Mind and Consciousness: Papers read at a Seminar held at the Ramakrishna Mission Institute of Culture, Kolkata, India on 16, 17 and 18 January 2004, 1290.

29. *The Panchatantra*, authored by Vishnu Sharma, is an ancient Indian collection of interrelated animal fables in Sanskrit verse and prose, arranged within a frame story.

30. Anna Freud significantly advanced the field of child psychoanalysis. She emphasized the importance of the ego and its defensive mechanisms.

31. During the Korean War (1950-53), the US carpet bombed North Korea, which were more bombs than the United States used against the Japanese during World War II.

32. William Shakespeare, *Troilus and Cressida*, Act 4: Scene 5.

33. Charles Robert Darwin was an English naturalist, geologist and biologist widely known for his contributions to evolutionary biology. His proposition that all species of life have descended from a common ancestor is now generally accepted and considered a fundamental concept in science.

34. Charles Darwin, *The Expressions of the Emotions in Man and Animals*, first published 1872, Oxford University Press (4th ed.), 2009.

35. Desmond Morris, *Manwatching: A Field Guide to Human Behaviour* (1977) or *Bodytalk: The Meaning of Human Gestures* (1994).

36. Paul Ekman is an American psychologist and professor emeritus at the University of California, San Francisco. He is a pioneer in the study of emotions and their relation to facial expressions. He was ranked 59th out of the 100 most cited psychologists of the twentieth century.

37. The Facial Action Coding System (FACS) is a system to taxonomize human movements by their appearance on the face,

based on a system originally developed by Paul Ekman and Wallace Friesen.

38. CMU is a global research university known for its world-class interdisciplinary programs: arts, business, computing, engineering, humanities.

39. The Salk Institute for Biological Studies is a scientific research institute located in the La Jolla community of San Diego, California, US. It is engaged in a wide range of research, including on aging, immunology, and cancer.

40. Tian et al., 2003; Littlewort et al., 2004.

41. Sextus Julius Frontinus was a prominent Roman civil engineer, author, soldier and senator in the late first century AD. He was a successful general under Domitian, commanding forces in Roman Britain and on the Rhine and Danube frontiers.

42. Greenleaf on Evidence part 5, section 29 note; related to Deuteronomy.

43. Mark A Godsey, "Rethinking the Involuntary Confession Rule: Toward a Workable Test for Identifying Compelled Self-Incrimination," *California Law Review* 92, no. 2 (2005): 488.

44. The Declaration was proclaimed by the United Nations General Assembly in Paris on 10 December 1948 (General Assembly resolution 217 A) as a common standard of achievements for all peoples and all nations. https://www.un.org/en/about-us/universal-declaration-of-human-rights. Last accessed August 25, 2019.

45. For someone facing criminal charges, pleading the Fifth means exercising their right to remain silent and not incriminate themselves.

46. Miranda v. Arizona, 384 U.S. 436 (1966).

47. Watts v. Indiana, 338 U.S. 49 (1949).

48. Nandini Satpathy v. P.L. Dani (AIR 1978 SC 1025).

49. Raffel v. United States, 271 U.S. 494 (1926); Berghuis v. Thompkins, 560 U.S. 370 (2010).

50. Magna Carta Libertatum (Medieval Latin for "the Great Charter of the Liberties"), commonly called the Magna Carta is a charter

of rights agreed to by King John of England at Runnymede, near Windsor, on 15 June 1215.

51. The body of Jewish civil and ceremonial law and legend comprising the Mishnah and the Gemara. There are two versions of the Talmud: Babylonian Talmud (which dates from the fifth century AD but includes earlier material) and the earlier Palestinian or Jerusalem Talmud.

52. MP Sharma v. Satish Chandra (AIR 1954 SC 300; 1954 SCR 1077).

53. Maqbool Hussain v. State of Bombay (1953 SCR 730; AIR 1953 SC 325).

54. Kalawati v. State of HP, 1953 SCR 546.

55. Section 50(1) holds, "Every police officer or other person arresting any person without warrant shall forthwith communicate to him full particulars of the offence for which he is arrested or other grounds for such arrest."

56. Section 303 CrPC: "Any person accused of an offence before a Criminal Court, or against whom proceedings are instituted under this Code, may of right be defended by a pleader of his choice."

57. DK Basu v. State of West Bengal (1997 (1) SCC 416).

58. Crowe v. Michael Crowe and others. Nos. 05-55467(2010), US Court of Appeals, Ninth Circuit.

59. Report by National Commission on Law Observance and Enforcement.

60. William Sargant, *Battle for the Mind: A Physiology of Conversion and Brainwashing* (1957).

61. The author of *The Black Banners: The Inside Story of 9/11 and the War against al-Qaeda* (2011)

62. AS Aubry, RR Caputo, *Criminal interrogation* (1980)

63. Ibid.

64. JT Dillon, *Questioning and Teaching: A Manual of Practice* (2004).

65. Hans Gustav Adolf Gross was an Austrian criminal jurist and criminologist, the "Founding Father" of criminal profiling. A

criminal jurist, Gross made his mark as the creator of the field of criminality. Throughout his life, Hans Gross made significant contributions to the realm of scientific criminology.

66. Stan B Walters, *Principles of Kinesic Interview and Interrogation* (CRC Press, 1996).

67. Robert F Royal, Steven R Schutt, *The Gentle Art of Interviewing and Interrogation: A Professional Manual and Guide* (Englewood Cliffs, NJ: Prentice-Hall, 1976), 65-66.

68. *Educing Information* (2006), last accessed February 5, 2024. https://www.birdmarella.com/wp-content/uploads/2022/05/Intelligence-Science-Board-2006.pdf

69. Sun Tzu, *The Art of War* (London: Amber Books, 2012).

70. A research experiment consisting of a two-week simulation of a prison environment, undertaken by Philip Zimbardo, Psychology professor at Stanford University in 1971, to study the effects of situation variables on participants' reactions and behaviour.

71. Ibid.

72. *Criminal Interrogation* (Aubry, Caputo).

73. *The Black Banners* (Soufan).

74. The Law of Requisite Variety states that the larger the variety of actions available to a control system, the larger the variety of perturbations it is able to compensate. F Heylighen and C Joslyn, "The Law of Requisite Variety," *Principia Cybernetica Web*, August 31, 2001. http://pespmc1.vub.ac.be/REQVAR.html

75. Jerry Richardson and Joel Margulis, *The Magic of Rapport: How You Can Gain Personal Power in Any Situation*, (Harbor Pub Co, 1981), 15-17.

76. *Principles of Kinesic Interview and Interrogation* (Walters).

77. Gunnar Berggren is a licensed psychologist and psychotherapist. He is Adjunct Lecturer at the Department of Psychology, Stockholm University.

78. Theodor Reik was a psychoanalyst who trained as one of Freud's first students in Vienna, Austria, and was a pioneer of lay analysis in the United States.

79. S Moston et al., "The Effects of Case Characteristics on Suspect Behaviour During Police Questioning," *British Journal of Criminology* 32 (1992): 23-40.

80. Confessions are construed as "arising through the existence of a particular relationship between the suspect, the environment and significant others within that environment" (Gudjonsson, 1992, p. 66).

81. Sally Lloyd-Bostock, *Psychology in Legal Contexts: Applications and Limitation* (Oxford Socio-Legal Studies book series) (Palgrave Macmillan, 1981), 67-84.

82. Douglas Walton, "The Interrogation as a Type of Dialogue," *Journal of Pragmatics* 35, no. 12 (2003): 1771-1802.

83. William Sargant, *Battle for the Mind: A Physiology of Conversion and Brainwashing* (1957).

84. Lowery versus the County of Riley, Case No 04-3101JTM.

85. Questioning and Teaching (Dillon).

86. Rudyard Kipling was an English novelist, short story writer, poet and journalist. His works of fiction include the *Jungle Book* duology, *Kim*, the *Just So* stories and many short stories.

87. Douglas Walton, 'The Interrogation as a Type of Dialogue'.

88. *The Gentle Art...* (Royal, Schutt).

89. Walton (2003).

90. *Criminal Interrogation* (Aubry, Caputo).

91. *The Gentle Art...* (Royal, Schutt).

92. *Detecting Lies and Deceit* (Vrij).

93. *Criminal Interrogation* (Aubry, Caputo).

94. The Cialdini Principle of Consistency states: "Once people make a decision, take a stand or perform an action, they will face an interpersonal pressure to behave in a consistent manner with what they have said or done previously".

95. John Richard Boyd was a United States Air Force fighter pilot and Pentagon consultant during the second half of the twentieth century. His theories have been highly influential in military, business and litigation strategies and planning.

96. *Go* is an abstract strategy board game for two players in which the aim is to capture more territory than the opponent by building

fortresses and fencing off empty space. The game was invented in China more than 2,500 years ago and is believed to be the oldest board game continuously played to the present day.

97. Among the "deep interrogation" methods used by the British, five techniques caused intense physical and psychological pain and suffering: deprivation of sleep, food and drink, stress positions, hooding and subjection to white noise.

98. The Landau Commission was a three-man Commission set up by the Israeli Government in 1987 to enquire into various interrogation methods used by the General Security Service (GSS).

99. Axel Dreher, Martin Gassebner and Lars-Hinrich Siemers, "Does Terrorism Threaten Human Rights? Evidence from Panel Data," *Journal of Law and Economics* 53, no. 1 (2010): 65-93.

100. Alison, Alison, Elntib and Noone, "ORBIT (Observing Rapport Based Interpersonal Techniques): A Manual for Assessing and Coding Interpersonal Rapport," Internal Document, University of Liverpool, UK (2010).

101. Ulrich Straus, *The Anguish of Surrender: Japanese POWs of World War II* (Seattle: University of Washington Press, 2004).

102. Samuel Huntington, *The Clash of Civilizations and Remaking of the World Order* (Penguin Random House, 2022).

103. *The Black Banners* (Soufan).

104. Carl von Clausewitz was a Prussian general and military theorist who stressed the "moral" and political aspects of waging war. His most notable work, *Vom Kriege*, though unfinished at his death, is considered a seminal treatise on military strategy and science.

105. *Criminal Interrogation* (Aubry, Caputo).

106. John Bodkin Adams was a British general practitioner, convicted fraudster and suspected serial killer. Between 1946 and 1956, 163 of his patients died while in comas. In addition, 132 out of 310 patients had left Adams money or items in their wills.

107. Harold Frederick Shipman was an English general practitioner and serial killer. He is considered to be one of the most prolific serial killers in modern history, with an estimated 250 victims.

108. Jeremy Bentham's theory of utilitarianism holds that pleasure and pain are linked to people's actions.

109. The US Army Field Manual on Interrogation, sometimes known by the military nomenclature FM 34-52, is a 177-page manual describing to military interrogators how to conduct effective interrogations while conforming with US and international law. It has been replaced by FM 2-22.3 Human Intelligence Collector Operations.

110. *The Black Banners* (Soufan).

111. Ibid.

112. José Padilla, also known as Abdullah al-Muhajir or Muhajir Abdullah, is a US citizen who was convicted in a federal court for aiding terrorists. Padilla was arrested in Chicago on May 8, 2002, on suspicion of plotting a radiological bomb attack.

113. Moston, note 195; also see Pearse et al.

114. Richard Leo, "Police Interrogations, False Confessions, and Alleged Child Abuse Cases," *University of Michigan Journal of Law Reform* 50, no. 3 (2017).

115. Phillips and Brown, 1998.

116. Leiken, 1970, 19-20.

117. The Convention on the Rights of the Child (CRC) was approved by the General Assembly of the United Nations on November 20, 1989.

118. The UN Standard Minimum Rules for the Administration of Juvenile Justice, commonly known as the Beijing Rules, were adopted by the UN General Assembly in November 1985. The resolution invited and requested member states to implement these rules in their respective juvenile justice legislation.

119. 1999 SCC 591.

120. The 2012 Delhi gang rape and murder, commonly known as the Nirbhaya case, involved a rape and fatal assault of a woman that occurred on December 16, 2012 in the Munirka area of Delhi.

121. Justice Stephen Breyer spoke on "Science in the Courtroom" at the Annual Meeting of the American Association for the Advancement of Science, 1998.

122. *Educing Information* (2006), last accessed January 25, 2024. https://groups.seas.harvard.edu/courses/ge157/educing.pdf

123. He along with David E Zulawski authored *Practical Aspects of Interview and Interrogation*, published by CRC Press in 1993.

124. Regarding Daubert v. Merrell Dow Pharmaceuticals (1993) 509 US 574 2786.

125. State v. Pitts, 62 Wn.2d 294 (1963).

126. Dinesh Dalmia v. State, Crl. R.C. No. 259 of 2006.

127. Criminal Writ Petition No.1924 of 2003 of Mumbai High Court.

128. "Fyre v. United States," *casetext*, 1923, last accessed December 2, 2023. https://casetext.com/case/frye-v-united-states-7.

129. Daubert v. Merrell Dow Pharmaceuticals (1993) 509 US 574 2786.

130. Criminal Appeal No 1267 of 2004 of SC.

131. Committee on Reforms of Criminal Justice System, Government of India, Ministry of Home Affairs, March 2003.

132. *Educing Information* (2006).

133. The murder of 12-year-old Stephanie Crowe took place in her home at Escondido, California, in January 1998. Stephanie's juvenile brother Michael and two other minors on interrogation made a confession, which later proved to be wrong.

134. The Central Park jogger case was a criminal case concerning the assault and rape of Trisha Meili, a woman in Central Park in Manhattan, New York, on April 19, 1989. The key suspects were five juveniles.

135. Ray Bull and Stavroula Soukara, "Four Studies of What Exactly Happens in Police interviews," in *Police Interrogations and False Confessions: Current Research, Practice and Policy Recommendations*, eds. G Daniel Lassiter and Christian A Meissner (Washington DC: American Psychology Association, 2010), 81-95.

136. Mark Costanzo and Allison Redlich, "Use of Physical and Psychological Force in Criminal and Military Interrogations." Google Books, last accessed February 5, 2024. https://scholar.

google.co.in/scholar?q=Costanzo+%26+Redlich,+2010%3B&h
l=en&as_sdt=0&as_vis=1&oi=scholart

137. The report details actions by CIA officials, including torturing prisoners, providing misleading or false information about classified CIA programs to the President, Department of Justice, Congress and the media, impeding government oversight and internal criticism and mismanaging the program.

138. Christian Meissner, Maria Hartwig and Melisssa Russano, "The need for a positive psychological approach and collaborative effort for improving practice in the interrogation room," *Law and Human Behaviour* 34, no. 1 (2010): 43-45, last accessed on February 20, 2024. https://psycnet.apa.org/record/2010-02823-005

139. *The Black Banners* (Soufan).

140. Ibid.

141. *Educing Information* (2006).

142. Ibid.

143. Committee on Reforms of Criminal Justice System Government of India, Ministry of Home Affairs, March 2003.

144. In public policy, a sunset clause is a measure within a statute, regulation or other law that provides that the law shall cease to have effect after a specific date, unless further legislative action is taken to extend the law.

145. "Law Commission Report No. 41: The Code Of Criminal Procedure, 1898 (Vol. 1)," *LatestLaws.com,* last accessed September 5, 2023. https://www.latestlaws.com/library/law-commission-of-india-reports/law-commission-india-report-no-41-code-criminal-procedure1898-vol-1/

146. "Historical Evolution of the Evidence," *Shodganga: A Reservoir of Indian Theses,* last accessed on August 12, 2023. https://shodhganga.inflibnet.ac.in/bitstream/10603/   148732/8/08_chapter%202.pdf

Bibliography

Books

Aubry, Arthur S and Rudolph *R Caputo. Criminal* Interrogation. Pennsylvania: Charles C Tho*mas, 1964.*

Darwin, Charles. The Expressions of the Emotions in Man and Animals. Oxford University Press, 2009 (1872).

Dillon, JT. Questioning *and Teaching: A Manua*l of Practice. Resource Publications, 2004.

Huntington, *Samuel. The Clash of Civilizations and Remaking of* the World Order. New York: Penguin Random House, 2022.

Peters, Edward. Torture: Expanded Edition. Philadelphia: University of Pennsylvania Press, 1996.

Royal, Robert F and *Steven R Schutt. The Gentle Art of Interviewing* and Interrogation: A Professional Manual and Guide. Engle*wood Cliffs, NJ: Prentice-Hall, 1976.*

Sargant, William. Battle for the Mind: A Physiology of Conversion and Brainwashing. Pelican Books, 1957.

*Solzhenitsyn, Aleksan*dr. The Gulag Archipelago. Paris: YMCA Press, 1973.

Soufan, Ali. The Black *Banners: The Inside Story of 9/11 and the War against al-*Qaeda. New York: Norton & Co, 2011.

Straus, Ulrich. The An*guish of Surrender: Japanese POWs of World War II Seattle: Univer*sity of Washington Press, 2004.

Tzu, Su*n. The Art of War. London: Amber Books Ltd, 2012.*

Vrij, Aldert. Detecting Lies *and Deceit: T*he Psychology of Lying and the Implications for *Professional Practice. New York: John Wiley and Sons, 2000.*

*Walters, Stan B. Principles of Kine*sic Interview and Interrogation. CRC Press, 1996.

Wickla*nder, Douglas and David E Zulawski. Practical Aspects* of Interview and Interrogation. CRC Press, 1993.

Articles in Journals/ Publications/ Documents

Alison, L et al. "ORBIT (Observing Rapport Based Interpersonal Techniques): A Manual for Asses*sing and Coding Inter*personal Rapport. Internal Document, University of Liverpool, UK (2010).

Cohen, Paul. "Torture and Translation in the Multilingual Courtrooms of Early *Modern France." Renaissance* Quarterly 69, no. 3 (2016): 899-939.

Dreher, Axel, Martin Gassebner and Lars-Hinrich Siemers. "Does Terrorism *Threaten Human Rights? Evidence from* Panel Data." Journal of Law and Economics 53, no.1 (2010): 65-93.

Educing Information: Interrogation: Art and Scien*ce. Intelligence* Science Board Phase I Report, National Defence Intelligence College. Washington DC: December 2006.

Kleinman, Stev*en. "The History of MIS-Y: U.S. Strategic In*terrogation during World War II." Master's thesis, Joint Military Intel*ligence College, August 2002.*

*Leiken, Lawrence S. "Police Interrogation in Colorado: The Implemen*tation of Miranda." Denver Law Journal 47, no. 1 (1970): 19-20.

Leo, Richard. "Police Interrogations, False Confessions, and Alleged Child Abuse Cases." University of *Michigan Journal of Law Refor*m 50, no. 3 (2017).

Meissner, Christian A and G Daniel Lassiter (eds.) Police Interrogations and False Confessions: Current Research, *Practice and Policy Recommendations. Washington DC*: American Psychology Association, 2010, 81-95.

Moston, S et al. "The Effects of *Case Characteristics* on Suspect Behaviour during Police Questioning." British Journal of Criminology 32 (1992): 23-40.

Pearse, J et al. "Police Interviewing and Psychological Vulnerabilities: Predicting the Likelihood of a Confession." Journal of Community and Applied Social Psychology 8, no. 1 (1998).

Peet, T Eric. "The Great Tomb Robberies of the Ramesside Age. Papyri Mayer A and B." The Journal of Egyptian Arch*aeology 2, no. 1 (1915): 204-206.*

Phillips, Coretta and David Brown. "Entry into the Criminal Justice System: A Survey of Police Arrests and their Outcomes." Home Office Research Study no. 185. London: HMSO, 1998.

Walton, Douglas. "The Interrogation as a Type of Dialogue." Journal of Pragmatics 35, no. 12 (2003): 1771-1802.

About the Author

K V Thomas has over 36 years of distinguished service in the Intelligence Bureau (IB), Ministry of Home Affairs, Government of India. He was awarded the President's Police Medal for Distinguished Service (2008) and the Indian Police Medal for Meritorious Service (1996) in recognition of his outstanding contributions. Thomas retired from the IB as Assistant Director in 2010. He is now fully engaged in producing quality publications in various subjects, especially internal security, enforcement, human rights and insurgency. He has authored seven books on such subjects.

JAICO PUBLISHING HOUSE

Elevate Your Life. Transform Your World.

ESTABLISHED IN 1946, Jaico Publishing House is home to world-transforming authors such as Sri Sri Paramahansa Yogananda, Osho, the Dalai Lama, Sri Sri Ravi Shankar, Sadhguru, Robin Sharma, Deepak Chopra, Jack Canfield, Eknath Easwaran, Devdutt Pattanaik, Khushwant Singh, John Maxwell, Brian Tracy, and Stephen Hawking.

Our late founder Mr. Jaman Shah first established Jaico as a book distribution company. Sensing that independence was around the corner, he aptly named his company Jaico ('Jai' means victory in Hindi). In order to service the significant demand for affordable books in a developing nation, Mr. Shah initiated Jaico's own publications. Jaico was India's first publisher of paperback books in the English language.

While self-help, religion and philosophy, mind/body/spirit, and business titles form the cornerstone of our non-fiction list, we publish an exciting range of travel, current affairs, biography, and popular science books as well. Our renewed focus on popular fiction is evident in our new titles by a host of fresh young talent from India and abroad. Jaico's recently established translations division translates selected English content into nine regional languages.

Jaico distributes its own titles. With its headquarters in Mumbai, Jaico has branches in Ahmedabad, Bangalore, Chennai, Delhi, Hyderabad, and Kolkata.

Visit our Website

Scan QR Code

www.ingramcontent.com/pod-product-compliance
Lightning Source LLC
LaVergne TN
LVHW010326200726
843507LV00010B/1381